I Ching

I Ching

BOOK OF CHANGES

Version for Optimism

A SYNTHESIS OF THE *I CHING* & POSITIVE PSYCHOLOGY

ALL READINGS PRESENTED IN THE POSITIVE
LIGHT OF OPPORTUNITY INHERENT IN YOUR
CURRENT SITUATION WITH THE WISDOM TO
REALIZE THE OPPORTUNITY
AND EVOLVE

Theo Cade, Ph.D.

To order additional copies of this book, contact:
Xlibris Corporation
1-888-795-4274
www.Xlibris.com
Orders@Xlibris.com
55763

CONTENTS

I want to thank my beloved sister, Claire, for introducing me to the *I Ching* in a moment of much-needed wisdom over thirty years ago. It served me well then and has ever since.

Thank you, Claire.

And thank you, dear friends, who read early drafts and recommended changes: Veronica Sheehan, Helena Buell, Mary Newswanger, Rick Mera, Marcella Burg, Suzi Butterfield, and Alana as channeled by Suzi.

Given wisdom with love,
opportunity arises in every situation.

TM

Above all pursue love and wisdom.

The greatest wisdom arises with self-study in relationship to your present situation. The *I Ching* reveals the essence of the situation together with wisdom about choices a wise person would make given the circumstances. Over time, the wisdom principles become a part of the student who thereby is increasingly evolving, transforming, eventually becoming a sage.

Integrating the principles of positive psychology empowers you to new levels of ability to synthesize ancient wisdom with current scientific knowledge, and create perspectives that generate positive self-fulfilling prophecies.

INTRODUCTION

Author's Commentary

This work is part of my calling to contribute to the realization of total permanent world peace and prosperity. It is my hope this *I Ching* contributes to the evolution of each us to take our part in this creation. The first step is to believe we can, to have an optimistic vision of the long-term evolution of humanity. As more of us hold this optimism, I believe it is and will increasingly be causal in the realization of our dreams coming true as a functional human family—the more, the sooner, the better. This requires our human belief, will, and action. We can each do our part evolving our own personal consciousness. This is my dream and vision for this *Version for Optimism* of the *I Ching*.

The first time I used the *I Ching* over thirty years ago, I had been unable to sleep for six nights in a row because of an inner conflict. My sister, Claire, suggested I consult the *I Ching* for guidance. At first, I was reluctant. I was uncomfortable getting a negative reading, but I was desperate and ready to try anything. So I did consult the *I Ching*.

That night I slept like a baby from the peace of mind I gained from the *I Ching*. Thereafter I used it often, and have received much valuable guidance to this day.

Over the years as I used the *I Ching*, I noticed that integrating the wisdom of positive psychology would add to this already rich resource. This is the essence of what you will find in this version of the *I Ching*. Readings from traditional texts sometimes increase anxiety, and may generate unnecessary negative, self-fulfilling prophecies. Readings from this *Version for Optimism* do the opposite while retaining the ancient wisdom and guidance inherent in each reading of the oracle.

I invite any and all who may be guided to find new ways to use or evolve this, or any other *I Ching,* or similar work to trust that leading and enjoy the contribution to humanity, deeper understanding, and personal fulfillment such endeavors bring.

The great psychologist, Carl Jung, studied and consulted the *I Ching* for thirty years. Jung explains his understanding of the oracle in his introduction to the classic Wilhelm/Baynes version of the *I Ching* published by Princeton University Press in 1950. In this writing, Jung laid the foundation for opening the western mind to enriching Eastern spiritual wisdom.

Divining

The *I Ching* is a serious spiritual text. Use of the *I Ching* is referred to as *divining* as distinct from *fortune telling.* Divining is seeking divine or spiritual guidance from an oracle. Approaching the *I Ching* with reverence leads to deep and valuable results. I would even go so far as to recommend not doing a reading until and if a reverent attitude is achieved. Traditional versions of the *I Ching* itself warn against using it lightly stating that one will not receive guidance sought when approached in an offhand way. In effect, if you play with it, it will play with you. I find it is best to allow your skepticism or cynicism to rest in active suspension of disbelief to allow an opportunity to gain real value.

When you consult the *I Ching,* you are able to tap into the animating force of the Universe, Spirit, if you will. The *I Ching* consistently communicates synchronistic readings for the reader who approaches it with sincerity. The readings are synchronistic in the sense that the most important aspect for the reader to consider at the time of the reading is revealed. Sometimes, rarely, I have found that I obtain readings that pertain not so much to the question I asked, but to my benefit, to some deeper question that was even more important for me to consider at the time.

I value direct experience over unsubstantiated belief. This direct, experiential learning is the meeting ground of empirical evidence and intuitive knowing. In this manner, we avoid the inherent error of limiting ourselves to only one or the other. The quality of my life, both inside and out, has vastly improved from openness to a mystical perspective, from opening to direct spiritual guidance. I find the *I Ching* particularly empowers this intuition.

For more commentary on the *I Ching* and topics like *Change and Time, Synchronicity and Randomness,* and *The Nature of Spirit and Relation to the Ego,* see my blog at *TheoCade.com.*

How to Consult the *I Ching*

To consult the *I Ching,* create a quiet, undisturbed time and place to contemplate the reading(s). Let its meanings gently become part of you. Apply the wisdom to yourself and your current concerns and delights. Over time you find yourself in an aura of calm wholeness. This sensation is Spirit enveloping you. Or perhaps Spirit is already and always there, and you are moving into states of consciousness where you experience Its presence.

This state of grace is the most benevolent and empowered state of consciousness to succeed at tasks before you, be they hard or easy, mundane or profound.

There are simple steps to obtain an I Ching reading. To make these instructions clearer, you will find answers to often repeated questions provided at the precise points the questions tend to arise. If you hold your questions of why to do each step until you read and visualize doing all the steps, your learning will be easier and faster.

The Best Way to Approach the *I Ching*

In a reverent state of being, focus on a question or circumstance you've chosen for contemplation.

Using the Coin-Toss Method

While there are a number of ways to access the *I Ching*, my own preference is the coin-toss method described below. For those who already have a coin toss or other method to divine a reading, staying with your original approach tends to yield the best results. If this is the case, you may choose to skip over these instructions.

To understand how to obtain an *I Ching* reading using the coin-toss method, it will be much easier if you read 1 through 6, below, before you throw the coins and mark the results.

1. Terms defined

To obtain an *I Ching* reading, it helps to be clear on terms: LINES, CHANGE LINES, TRIGRAMS, and HEXAGRAMS.

LINES are either a yin symbol ▬ ▬ or a yang symbol ▬▬▬. Yin is receptive. Yang is creative.

CHANGE LINES are lines that change from Yang to Yin or Yin to Yang.

TRIGRAMS are three lines stacked vertically. For example,

▬ ▬
▬▬▬
▬ ▬

HEXAGRAMS are six lines stacked vertically. *Hex* means six. Notice that each Hexagram is made of a lower and upper trigram. For example,

▬ ▬
▬▬▬
▬ ▬
▬▬▬
▬ ▬
▬▬▬

2. Throwing the coins

You determine each line by tossing three coins. Choose coins that each have a head and a tail side. This means, when it is time, you will throw the three coins once, then mark the result. Throw all three coins again, for a total of six times.

Each time you throw the three coins, mark the result as shown in number 3 below. Record the lines from the bottom up, as in Chinese writing and as a tree grows. The bottom line is line 1; the second from the bottom is line 2, and so on up to line 6, the top line.

3. Lines

Tossing three coins, there are four possible outcomes:

> Two heads and one tail
> Two tails and one head
> Three heads
> Three tails

LINES THAT DO NOT CHANGE

> Two heads and one tail is a — — yin line
> Two tails and one head is a ——— yang line

CHANGE LINES

> Three heads is a ——— yang line that changes to a yin — — line
> Three tails is a — — yin line that changes to a yang ——— line

The following table helps clarify how to record and read the results of your coin tosses.

	1st Hexigram Record as	1st Hexagram Read as		2nd Hexagram Record and Read as
3 heads	✳	———	changes to	– –
3 tails	–O–	– –	changes to	———
2 heads 1 tail	– –	– –	remains	– –
2 tails 1 head	———	———	remains	———

Table 1. How to record and read coin-toss results

4. Interpreting change lines

Because the *I Ching* helps navigate the constant changes in life, another name for the *I Ching* is *Book of Changes*.

To get a feel for change lines, reflect upon the following—when a pendulum swings to the end of an arc in one direction, it then heads back in the opposite direction.

Change lines indicate the momentum or energy in one direction is shifting to its opposite, from yang to yin, or from yin to yang.

Three heads or three tails are the extreme number of heads or tails you can obtain when you toss three coins. So we need a way to indicate these changes. In the convention we are using, here is how it is done.

Three heads are recorded ✳, meaning it will be read first as a ———
yang line, and second as a yin line — — .

Three tails are recorded ⊙, meaning it will be read first as a — —
yin line and second as a yang line ——— .

Three heads or three tails are thus called change lines.

Continue to read and clarity will come.

HOW TO PROCEED WHEN YOU GET CHANGE LINES

Whenever your coin toss includes three heads or three tails in any of
the six lines of the hexagram, you will have two hexagrams to read.

When your coin toss includes no lines with three heads or three tails,
you will have only one hexagram to read.

Remember, the first line is the bottom line. Record from the bottom
up. See Table 2 for example.

		1st Hexgram to Record	1st Hexgram to Read		2nd Hexgram to Record & Read
6th Line	2 heads 1 tail	− −	− −	remains	− −
5th Line	2 tails 1 head	−−−	−−−	remains	−−−
4th Line	2 heads 1 tail	− −	− −	remains	− −
3rd Line	2 tails 1 head	−−−	−−−	remains	−−−
2nd Line	3 tails	−O−	− −	changes to	−−−
1st Line	3 heads	−✕−	−−−	changes to	− −

Table 2. Example coin tosses with change lines

Notice Lines 1 and 2 changed from the first to the second hexagram, while lines 3, 4, 5, and 6, remained the same.

Remember, when you have no lines with three heads or three tails, you will have only one hexagram to read.

To repeat for clarity:

*If you do have three heads or three tails in any line, keep the
lines that are not three heads or three tails the same in the second
hexagram as in the first.*

*If you do not have any change lines with three heads or three tails,
you will have only one hexagram.*

For example, see Table 3.

		Hexagram to Record & Read	
6th Line	2 heads 1 tail	-- --	
5th Line	2 tails 1 head	——	
4th Line	2 heads 1 tail	-- --	No second hexagram because no lines change.
3rd Line	2 tails 1 head	——	
2nd Line	2 heads 1 tail	-- --	
1st Line	2 tails 1 head	——	

Table 3. Example coin tosses with no change lines

5. Trigram meanings

As mentioned above, trigrams are three lines stacked vertically like this:

Arranging yin - - and yang ——— lines in all possible combinations of three stacked vertically in trigrams, there are eight and only eight possibilities. Each trigram has a symbolic meaning.

Creative, Heaven

Energizing, Thunder

Open Space, Water

Keeping Still, Mountain

Receptive, Earth

Gentle, Wind, Wood

Connecting, Fire

Joyous, Lake

Table 4. The eight trigrams and their meanings

6. Throw the coins and look up the results

Now is the time to throw the coins and mark the results. Remember, the first coin throw is recorded as the bottom line. Record lines from the bottom up.

Two trigrams stacked one above the other form a hexagram:

To look up the number of a hexagram use the Hexagram Key at the end of this section. Look up the lower trigram on the vertical axis on the left side. Look up the upper trigram on the horizontal axis across the top. Find the box where the two intersect. The number in this box is the number of your reading. Turn to that reading in the book, and contemplate your question or subject of focus in the light of what you read.

There is one more use of change lines. At the end of each reading, there are six lines, numbered 1 to 6. Read only the change lines that correspond to the change lines you received in your first hexagram.

The second hexagram, created by the change lines, never has change lines to read or to create another hexagram.

Remember, Line 1 is at the bottom of your hexagram and line 6 is the top line. These lines give you additional information to contemplate specific to your question.

Hexagram Key

For convenience, this chart is also on the last page before the back cover.

Upper ▶ Lower ▼	Heaven	Thunder	Water	Mountain	Earth	WindWood	Fire	Lake
Heaven	1	34	5	26	11	9	14	43
Thunder	25	51	3	27	24	42	21	17
Water	6	40	29	4	7	59	64	47
Mountain	33	62	39	52	15	53	56	31
Earth	12	16	8	23	2	20	35	45
WindWood	44	32	48	18	46	57	50	28
Fire	13	55	63	22	36	37	30	49
Lake	10	54	60	41	19	61	38	58

The Structure of the Readings

In this, *I Ching, Version for Optimism,* each reading contains first the number and name followed by an affirmation that represents the essence of the reading. Then the hexagram appears, consisting of two trigrams, with names of the upper and lower trigram. The reading itself comes next. Finally, when you have change lines, there is an affirmation for each change line.

Making a daily routine of writing the affirmation on a card to carry with you and refer to often during your day, brings the wisdom of the reading to the many choices you make in a day. The inner states achieved from the choices you are making over time, bring about your spiritual evolution.

Use the *I Ching* to access Divine guidance and let life itself evolve you with pure love.

Enjoy.

1. CREATING HEAVEN

I align with the primary power
creating heaven inside and out.

 Creative, Heaven
Creative, Heaven

This is a time of empowered creating. You are empowered by the ultimate Source. This is not mere theoretical or cognitive understanding. With authentic openness, you are in direct dialogue with the essence of life itself. Approaching the *I Ching* with an open mind, you come to experience synchronicities that lend confidence in spiritual reality and its presence each here and now. Over time you experience that which is alive in the *I Ching* is one with that Source which is always present, good, knowing, and powerful. With this empowerment, you evolve as a co-creator with life itself.

This first reading, *Creating Heaven*, in combination with the second, *Be Receptive and Nurture*, reflect the two primary forces of the universe, creating and receiving, yang and yin. They are the fundamental elements of the *I Ching*. Personal evolution occurs in stages of transforming lower nature to higher nature, evolving thought, feeling, attitude, and action. Here you are involved with the more purely creative. Creative momentum for personal evolution unites you with divine will. Your fulfilled self wants to contribute to the well-being of the world around you, its people, and other living beings, including the earth itself.

An empowered way to use this creative force for self evolution is to "make your subjective experience an object of study".[1] Your existence improves immeasurably as does your world, in concert with your evolved state, actions, and peaceful presence.

Spirit supports you and specifically communicates information, wisdom, synchronicities, sensing, feelings, and even, at times, by voice as clearly as though someone were speaking directly to you. To intuit messages from Source, your part is to stay open and clear of negativity. You grow by releasing destructive, pain-inducing tendencies, and cultivating constructive ones. Reverent listening inside and sensing outside open pathways to receive the gifts always coming to you. As a spiritual practice to enhance your ability to receive, spiritual guidance and receptivity create the joy of purity.

As you create in concert with the Divine, you succeed and are fulfilled. And you know when non-action is more beneficial than action. You experience fulfillment after fulfillment. Greater gifts come as you give. You find profound personal peace. Happiness arises not from being pursued directly, rather spontaneously from serving others in love.

Success viewed as *what's in it for me* is distinguished from fulfillment, which speaks to contribution for the good of the whole. Success is good when integrated with fulfillment. And comparing the two, success is nothing compared to fulfillment.

Remaining on a spiritual creative path creates ultimate infinite joy. A holy presence envelops you. You are happy with what is and what you know will be. You feel your soul's purpose being fulfilled. There is no hurry. Each state has its rewards and wisdom to be savored before letting go into the next. You experience divine existence, here and now, each moment.

Welcome to heaven. Since we are all connected to the stream of life, creating pure joy for others centers you in heavenly existence. The more you evolve, the more heavenly experience deepens for you.

There is variety in the Creative, Heaven. Part of the path is not hurrying through the value in each experience. Savoring each step creates real value for you, your loved ones, your human family, and the family of all life. Stay present and responsive to divine intuition. The experience of complete oneness is wholly yours in its best timing.

Now is a time to be active in creating your own heavenly being. One way to support positive, self-fulfilling prophesy is to repeat the thought, "I am a lighthouse, not a weathervane."[2] Enjoy.

LINE 1: The time is not ripe to act. For the present, be confident and self-contained. Wait to act until it is clear what to do, and when. In the meantime, know your goodness and ultimately things work out fine.

I wait for the right time to do the right thing.

LINE 2: Your light is bright. You distinguish yourself in dedication and spontaneous focus. As yet, others do not consciously know this; soon they will know. While you wait, consult the infinite within through the *I Ching,* or other sacred means like meditation. These actions carry you forward.

I stay aligned with the Divine and know great things are coming.

LINE 3: You are beginning to receive acclaim for greatness as a result of your inner work. Be careful not to be swept up in these external acknowledgments and lose the inner connection that created them. Stay focused within, and you continue to reap what is most valuable.

I taste the initial success of inner evolution. To continue, I avoid arrogance, stay connected within, and keep growing.

LINE 4: You have a choice. Because of creative depth, you can enter the external world and effect progress, or you can pursue deeper inner development. After achieving a level of excellence and integrating both inner and outer, each reinforces the other as when one teaches and learns at a deeper level.

I may focus on evolving within or contributing to the external world. When the time is ripe, I integrate the two and both advance.

LINE 5: You have reached heavenly realms. Without trying, you create benevolent results. Stay connected to the innocent, pure, and good, and you will continue to prosper in all ways.

As I evolve, I experience good spontaneously arising. To keep good coming, I remain united with the greater good.

LINE 6: When you achieve a level of success, temptation to overstep your abilities leads to a fall. Arrogance creates the falling. Continued humility and openness to learning prevent this decline, and increasing success continues.

As I continue the humble openness that brought me this far, good keeps coming.

2. Be Receptive And Nurture

*Like the earth, I am receptive and
nurturing.*

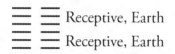 Receptive, Earth
Receptive, Earth

Receive and nurture all, like the earth. Bring the same level of enthusiasm in nurturing and receiving as you do to creating. You will be fulfilled. Your heart will overflow with love. Your life will flourish. Put yourself in the hands of wise, kind ones. Be wise and kind yourself. You expand exponentially when you put the same attention into serving others as you would yourself.

Whatever events occur, embrace the unfolding. Embrace as a mother embraces her growing children. In a sense, your circumstances are your children. Each life event is a gift, either pure and simple, or an opportunity for growth. Some gifts are pleasant, some neutral, and some challenging. When challenging gifts arrive, remember your higher self sent them for your expansion. Embrace all your children. They become mature adults who return the nurturing they received in your hands.

Sometimes we react with injured innocence to circumstances or people in ways that get us caught in reactive emotions like anger, hatred, greed, jealousy, or obsessing. There is a way to dissolve the feelings.

Simply ask yourself who it is that is experiencing being injured. Then quietly experience the experiencer.[3]

Be more than do. Let go of the burden of control. Yield. Recognize and receive wise counsel from all sources. Allowing others to choose and decide returns the same freedom to you. Others are honored by respectful attention and return the honoring. With such mutuality, you come to call each other friend.

Discern and follow the path of greatest wisdom through study and contemplation. To serve best, support all about you. Participate joyfully. Follow the good, beautiful, and true. Your days will be filled with goodness, wisdom, and kindness.

LINE 1: You are beginning to take a negative perspective. Return to the positive. Your actions and creations will go well.

I recognize negativity arising in me and transform it early.

LINE 2: Be quiet and inward. Particularly when in the dark, one must feel the right path; this right path feels wise, kind, soft, and caring. Feel and follow the right path. You will succeed.

I sense within to feel and follow the wise and gentle path.

LINE 3: To retain independence by avoiding fame is not wisdom. True worth and self-love come from fulfilling your unique destiny. Yet to be independent and free, you can still work in private.

I stay free and independent, not by avoiding fame, but by honoring my privacy.

LINE 4: Pushing ahead brings negative consequences as does giving in. Whether alone or in a crowd, be reserved now. Be still, quiet, and whole. Be more contemplative than expressive for now. Then you weather this time well.

I hold back now for later benefit.

Line 5: In your heart, mind, and will, find, integrate, and follow the good.

I find the good in my heart and follow it in my mind, will, and action.

Line 6: Let serving the good be your guiding principle. Light cancels dark. When they meet, only light remains. Resist not the dark; simply embrace the light. Go directly for good, not against bad. If you resist, you become too much like what you resist. Take each step humbly, harmonizing others interests with your own. Peace of mind comes with shining light on others and shining light within yourself.

I cancel dark with light, including the light of humility.

3. New Beginnings

*I begin anew
with care, constancy, and joy.*

 Open Space, Water
Energizing, Thunder

Water from above energizes new life below. A new seed bursts open. A blade of grass pushes up through the earth, sensing obstacles, and flexibly bending around them. With time and flow, the grass matures and becomes abundant. You are nurturing new life.

You are beginning new creations. Replace fear and worry with caution, constancy, humility, and joy. Be like the wise farmer who prepares the land well, plants healthy seeds in sufficient and well-placed space to grow. Tend the soil and infant crops with exquisite attention, doing the best at each stage. Proceed with the self-confidence born of such care.

To avoid unnecessary disappointments, align with nature. You cannot will a seed to grow faster than its time. Go slowly; this is beautiful. Embracing challenge promotes growth. Attentiveness, sunshine, water, soil nutrients, and protection from harm support small seeds blooming into abundance. Patient, wise perseverance shifts challenge to opportunity. With opportunity, constancy generates greatness.

As you begin, open to what's needed. Enroll excellent assistance. Take pleasure in life. Appreciate space, air, and time to be. Savor your existence. Tend projects. Take each step at the right moment. Enjoy allowing your warm-hearted nurturing instincts. To blossom, let life live.

Nature nurtures you when you unite with it. Trust the inner impetus for growth. Just be, without pushing. Allow Spirit to guide your actions. You will fulfill your soul mission.

Today's detour could be tomorrow's desired destination. Embracing challenge with good cheer brings you beyond wants and needs. Harvest the gift in the challenge. Dreams come true. All it takes is patience, perseverance, and appreciation of the good people and things present in your life now. Appreciation, gratitude, and praise begin quietly inside and create constant growth into your higher self. No need for extra work or words because who you are is so attractive that life loves you.

LINE 1: Getting started can be frustrating. Stay humble. Attract excellent assistance and assistants. Persevere. Proceed with steady calm attention and an open and modest attitude.

I accept initial frustrations and persevere with equanimity.

LINE 2: As you begin to realize your dreams, challenges occur. Others arrive with help or relief, but some do not fit your ultimate visions. Be wary of accepting assistance that would lead you off course. Wait for the right assistance. You will know the rightness by your experience of wholeness.

I discern and focus my time and attention intuitively. I sense the best and let go of the rest.

LINE 3: You are unable to proceed because you need new competencies or authority. Apparent blocks to progress provide helpful information about your most valuable focus. Obtain what's needed, and you will succeed.

I embrace the implicit guidance of apparent blocks to progress. I manage the situation well and proceed with well-deserved confidence.

LINE 4: Don't resist what's needed. Embrace it. Do things well and in sequence. With excellent timing and assistance, all will be well. Be humble, patient, and attend to each detail willingly and carefully.

I persevere with the patience for excellence that guarantees success.

LINE 5: Excellence and completion come in stages. Little successes are better than big failures. Big failures come from overreaching. The best way to proceed is step by step with humility. Over time little successes lead to big dreams coming true.

I create the little successes that make big dreams come true.

LINE 6: When difficulties arise, you may be tempted to give up. This would be sad and unnecessary. One of the best things in life is to persevere by developing slowly. Constant improvement with goodwill creates profound evolution, empowerment, and realized dreams.

I persist and let challenges inform and thereby assist my progress.

4. DIVING IN

*I dive into challenges
with optimum open-minded enthusiasm
and calm nonattachment.*

Keeping Still, Mountain
Open Space, Water

D ive into life with the open-minded enthusiasm of a small child. To create the open mind needed to succeed, dive into the complexities of new situations with a positive attitude and equanimity by keeping still within like a powerful mountain. Embrace enthusiasm without attachment.

Enthusiasm, without attachment, generates great gifts. Enthusiasm, without attachment, brings learning and growth through openness to new experience. Enthusiasm, without attachment, creates freedom to explore without inner demands that things be any certain way. Enthusiasm, without attachment, is valuable when exploring new things because in their newness, you have less ability to predict or control precisely what will happen. You expand. You create new adventures. You increase your wisdom, skills, and riches.

Enthusiasm, without attachment, allows for including others with energy to inspire their participation and flexibility to acknowledge and integrate their good ideas and varying styles and values.

With humility, there can be enthusiasm without attachment. Humility prevents emotional reactivity. Humility lowers expectations, bringing peace of mind, learning, competence, and positive relationships. An open, enthusiastic beginner's mind frees you from the emotional reactions of thwarted expectations. Being willing to not know and not succeed right away, and still proceed is a noble act rewarded by growing wisdom, fulfillment, and joy.

As you begin new things, expect challenges; embrace them. Embracing challenge is the taproot of learning and growing. Be prepared to reverse, rethink, and redo steps that do not function well at first. This open-minded redoing gains knowledge from what did not go well at first. We are all pioneers in our own lives, constantly discovering improvements. Embracing challenge builds wisdom, will, strength, and enjoyment.

When things get harder and stress increases, our tendency may be to try to decrease the discomfort by pushing harder and faster. Further, we may choose to look away from or even deny the source of the stress in an effort to bring comfort. Slowing down, rather than speeding up, can shift us to a more empowered awareness and reduce the stress. Slower is faster. With a more relaxed pace, we can concentrate better and even move into a genius zone where intuitive brilliance emerges. As we experience conquering previously impenetrable problems, joy springs forth in the experience of our growth and increased ability.

Keeping faith that all things can be directed for good helps realize this. Life provides challenging experiences that can enhance you. Having an open attitude harmonizes you with challenge and makes the gifts real.

Acceptance, embracing new experiences with innocence, detachment, and non-expectation are primary principles of the *I Ching*. Be enthusiastically receptive to each experience with the faith of a small child. The power of positive self-fulfilling prophecy comes with acceptance and transforms you in stages, from beginner to master. You enhance skills, peace of mind, relationships, and joy in the short, medium, and long run.

Open to life; dive in. Look, listen, learn, and grow as you explore the new.

LINE 1: Be sober and self-disciplined. Yet do not overdo this and inhibit adventure, joy, and love. Optimum is less than maximum, and more than minimum.

I jump in with joy and non-expectation, neither over, nor under doing it.

LINE 2: Grace and humility create success. When relating to one who is obviously uninformed or misguided, be gracious and humble. The kindness of holding back outwardly comes from inner strength.

When relating to one who is just learning, I draw on inner strength and remain graciously humble.

LINE 3: A calm approach with neither too much, nor too little enthusiasm facilitates full functioning.

I remain calm with neither too much, nor too little enthusiasm.

LINE 4: Be guided and motivated by living into your dreams coming true. You will realize your dreams and enjoy the journey.

I am motivated and guided by living into my dreams coming true.

LINE 5: As you seek and find new ways to fulfill your heart's desires, be joyfully open like a small child, and wisely calm like an elder. By trusting in life and doing your part carefully and well, you joyfully fulfill your dreams.

I proceed with the joyful enthusiasm of a small child and the calm wisdom of an elder.

LINE 6: Erroneous ways lead to erroneous results. Master yourself, and allow life to lead others to their own mastery. Gentle yet firm self-discipline and self-correction keep you progressing. Allow life to tame others; it will. Allowing others to be affected by the circumstances they create frees you from carrying the learning opportunities that truly belong to others. This stance improves the quality of their learning, your relationship with them, and your life.

I enjoy the fruits of mastering myself and allow life to lead others to their own self-mastery.

5. High Consciousness While Waiting

I embrace life
creating a delectable present and future.

 Open Space, Water
Creative, Heaven

You realize your dreams as you hold heavenly creative visions that all will be well as you flow like water through challenges. Excellence takes time. It happens in stages. Savor the excellence you are creating with patience and pleasure. Nurture yourself as you wait.

Bear with whatever has yet to be completed in a spirit of joy and self-confidence. Like attracts like. As you embrace the good, the beautiful, and the true, good embraces you. Trust in divine will. Open your heart and mind to what's good, beautiful, and true. You will be creating your own earthly heaven.

Honor others' freedom to make peace with life. If you are part of what others need to make peace with, the best course of action is to hold these others firmly and fairly in goodwill and inner light until they resolve their issues in their own timing.

Allow others their own feelings without resisting, blaming, or trying to fix them. When you have compassion for them, they have compassion for you.

Enjoy the feast of life as you wait. Congratulations, you are approaching completion of current challenges. As you follow the principle of feasting while you wait, you complete everything necessary, sooner and better.

LINE 1: Good news. Things are going to go at a normal pace for a time. Continue to be present, and enjoy this interlude by doing normal productive things. Such relaxing, yet creative openness, better prepares you for any later challenges that may come along. Until then, know that you, your life, and your circumstance are and will be fine. Such quiet confidence feeds health and endurance.

I self-confidently enjoy, feast, and flow with careful excellence as I await the ripening of my dreams coming true.

LINE 2: One may feel uncertain ground underfoot with potential problems. The most powerful thing affecting you now is the meaning you choose to give events. Let go of doubt and fear. Return to calm and presence in the moment. Do not let others test you by sowing doubt in your mind. Keep still inwardly and self-reliant outwardly. Others leave you in peace. You create your own equanimity. All is well.

I replace doubt with optimistic self-reliance.

LINE 3: Free yourself from negative thinking. This prevents negative self-fulfilling prophecy. Further, take responsibility to create positive self-fulfilling prophecy. Constantly open yourself to higher possibilities. You will transform negative situations into positive learning opportunities.

I embrace positive self-fulfilling prophecy.

LINE 4: To deal well with any particularly challenging moment, use all you know to be good, right, and true. Reverent humility invokes the assistance of all including the Divine. The quiet, inner stillness of deep meditation clears the field. Replacing reactivity with calm, wise, conscious responding, you remain whole through resolution. You come out the other side more inspired, wise, and successful.

I attract the support of others and the Divine through reverent humility.

LINE 5: This is a moment of respite in the midst of challenges. Take advantage of the peaceful time to build strength. Also build confidence that all will be well. Let go of demanding that everything be done at once and thereby unnecessarily exhausting yourself. Enjoy steps unfolding one by one, naturally. Create phases in projects, and enjoy the delectable completion of each phase in its best timing. Before you know it, you will find yourself through the whole thing with the great enjoyment of inner and outer reward.

I savor steps to completion.

LINE 6: At first events seem unfavorable, but they turn out better than the best you could have imagined. Sometimes what looks like a negative occurrence turns out to be just the change needed for progress. Keep an open mind. Persevere in calm, quiet inner connection to the light. Opportunities arise from seemingly unrelated events. Embrace life as it comes, and it will embrace you, even when what you expected or yearned for turns out differently. Be the creative force in your own life. Align with your higher self, with your loving wisdom and power, and all will go extremely well for you now.

I embrace each event as it enfolds, knowing that in doing so I create the best possible path and destination.

6. TRANSFORMING CONFLICT

I transform conflict by focusing on good and letting the rest be.

 Creative, Heaven
Open Space, Water

You bring about heaven on earth by flowing like water out of problems. This is good news because it means the conflict may be resolved. Ultimately, all conflict is inner conflict. Inner resolution transforms outer conflict. You are free to choose how you approach conflict. Your choice determines your success.

Conflict arises with the presence of both thesis and antithesis. Resolution arises from combining the two in dynamic tension to create synthesis, which becomes the new, higher level thesis. The way to creating this higher level synthesis is to include what was constructive and transcend what was destructive in the original thesis and antithesis. This synthesis becomes the new thesis.

Experiencing yourself as a creator rather than a victim resolves inner conflict and ultimately outer conflict. Empower yourself; ask, *"Why do good things always happen to me?"* which produces a blessed identity. Then ask, *"How can I contribute?"* By focusing on these two questions, you give yourself a creator identity.

This does not mean to avoid protecting yourself when necessary, not with violence, but by withdrawing to a nurturing time and place. From this nurturing place, encourage disarming on all sides. This means coming from a creator mind-set when protecting yourself rather than a victim mind-set. When you contemplate how you can contribute, ways to proceed may arise indirectly. When you ask, *How can I contribute,* worry decreases and effective action increases. Over time decreased worry and increased effective action use the energy of the initial conflict to create constructive conditions and feelings. You also see what is right for you to do in the situation without diluting your effectiveness by taking on too much.

Coming from the *how can I contribute* perspective puts you in a frame of mind that enhances relationships.

Another way conflict occurs is when you want to change someone else who cannot or does not want to change and probably won't change. Pushing against others entrenched in a position strengthens their resistance. To maintain balance, their instinctive response is to push back. When you allow others room to be as they are and find their own way, life nudges them upward at just the right rate for their optimal growth. This opens the possibility for conflict resolution within you and between both of you. To remove this inner growth stress robs another of the motivation to shift. Things often work out for the best when you allow others to be as they are.

So too with yourself. Accepting yourself to be just who you are frees you from self-judgment and consequent impulses toward denial through self-destructive activities such as addictions. This opens the heavenly path of constant self-improvement. By feeling and accepting your feelings, you allow life's natural influences to energize your growth. You open yourself to inspiration by attracting constructive forces. You put yourself in the empowered position of choosing to keep or shift your perspective depending upon whether or not you are nurtured or experiencing pain.

If your automatic response is to blame, get angry, or choose a victim role, you can change your automatic response by accepting the challenge of learning and growing, and thus become more effective and joyful in life.

Positive attraction is more beneficial than self-punishment. To be sure, self-discipline is beneficial, but it works best with the positive perspective of approaching good rather than self-oppression. The self-inspiration of positive perspectives leads to wholeness, joyfully moving you toward worthy goals.

Because you have free will, you have choice in how to resolve conflicts. Evolving yourself is the better way. This transforms issues into learning experiences. Evolving yourself gives others room to resolve their conflicts, inspiring them as they see your success. Supporting others' freedom wins their goodwill.

Respecting others' free will to resolve their own challenges in their own way in loving support is best for everyone. This frees you and others. Accepting and allowing is loving. Burdens that are rightfully others' are lifted from your shoulders. This shapes their growth positively, just as accepting and allowing your own challenges shapes your growth in positive ways.

Discern if you want to stay closely connected to another. Some relationships are so dear, and the other so willing and capable of resolution, that effort to resolve conflicts with them consistently holds high promise. Other relationships, without the prerequisite goodwill, are more harmonious when kept at a wise distance. Disengaging lovingly may be the better thing to do.

How you approach others determines your success in resolving conflicts. Exquisite timing supports harmonious resolutions. Determine if others are willing and capable to receive and respond positively to your requests at a given time. Ask, *will this communication serve the greater good now?* If it will, proceed. At times, others' inner issues may distract them; allow them time and room to resolve within and reengage at a more opportune time.

Because we each have free will, which is a good thing, you have most power with yourself and least power with others. Understand your own values and wants clearly. Similarly, have compassion for others' values and wants too. You are more likely to succeed by correcting yourself than correcting others. With an attitude of compassion and goodwill for others and yourself, request their support. For example, gently ask for quiet when you are ill or overwhelmed, rather than judging the other as rude and noisy and telling them all about their faults.

Avoid the approach to circumstances that you will only be whole when someone else changes and this person is either unwilling or unable to change. When this is true, approaching conflict by resolving within is a powerful and better way to resolution.

When it is imperative that you exercise your power of choice, the more agreeably you disagree, the better your opportunities for successful resolution. A way to increase the likelihood of harmonious resolution is to begin by agreeing to co-create consensus where each party benefits in mutual goodwill, trust, and respect. It helps, at the outset, to agree that no definitive action will be taken until all parties agree. Simply put, agreeing that any plan of action takes a *yes* from each party before being carried out supports success. When working to agree to resolve conflict, it helps to be open to new ideas for resolution.

When there is strong reason to resolve past conflict and you know or sense the other is holding resentment toward you, an effective path to resolution is to approach the other with compassion, goodwill, and understanding for their perspective. Then proceed slowly and carefully to learn the part you contributed to the conflict. What could you have done better? Begin by expressing that you want to resolve the issue and acknowledge what you now know you could have done better. If in response you receive judgments of you from the other in a disarming tone, ask for ideas on what you could have done better, instead of judgments and negative feedback.

Love and great relationships come from how we feel about ourselves in each other's presence. Harmoniously resolving conflict adds trust. Bonds of affection are deepened and preserved. Everybody wins.

Integrating the principles in this reading empower you to transform conflict to benefit.

LINE 1: At the beginning, when a conflict is small, the best way to resolve it is to let it go. This helps particularly if the other has greater power or is extremely reactive. Moving on to more productive things creates the greatest good.

I let go of conflict while it is still small.

LINE 2: Pushing back creates more of what you do not want. Withdrawing harmoniously, allowing, and proceeding in peace resolves issues beyond your scope and skill.

I resolve conflict by allowing others to be where they are.

LINE 3: Creating good work is far more valuable than recognition. Focus on the former and let go of the latter. You will succeed.

I focus on good work, not recognition.

LINE 4: Following what is beautiful, good, and true ultimately empowers you. Creating harmony with others is the best. Then you will know serenity and success. Just because you may be bigger and stronger does not mean you should pursue a conflict. In a lower position, humble dignity wins support from those at all levels. When in a position of power, what you do may have even stronger effects. Now humble dignity is even more beneficial to you and all others.

In all positions, especially powerful ones, I proceed with humble dignity, to support resolution and serenity.

LINE 5: Consulting a wise, objective, and influential person for arbitration helps resolve a conflict. The good and right are supported.

I seek wise guidance for resolution.

LINE 6: Attention to an issue increases conflict now. Withdrawal resolves the conflict quickly and completely. Break through to self-evolution. Let go of negativity. Come from your higher nature. Form constructive perspectives. Create all win. Ask not, *"why am I so mistreated,"* which creates a victim identity; rather ask *"how can I contribute,"* and thereby be a creator.

I understand that sometimes letting go of an issue can be the best way to resolve it; this may be one of those times.

7. Leadership By High Self

I lead from my higher self.

 Receptive, Earth
Open Space, Water

Water within the earth is stored up power. Tap the positive power within yourself and others. Leading others with generous open kindness inspires loyalty, enthusiasm, and good work. The best way to create excellent visions and fulfill them is to include others in the process. Co-creativity inspires. Yet avoid overindulging and excessive unproductive inputs.

Choose better paths to higher goals. All goes well when you lead what's lower with your higher nature in healthy self-discipline.

Build motivation and action on a firm foundation. Taking care within elevates all without. Proceed with equanimity. Move at an optimum pace. Get sufficient rest. Eat well. Embrace what is better, kinder and more creative. You bring the better into being. Connection to Spirit deepens inner resources. Regular quiet inner awareness creates calm, whole, centered leadership. You benefit yourself and your world.

Experiencing your own live center; you connect to the center of all life, to the source of healing, health, and wholeness. Congratulations, you are creating great things as you stay connected to and lead from your high self.

LINE 1: Set the highest intentions. Before beginning, be sure your purpose is good. Be organized and coordinated with others. Proceed with humility.

Before beginning, I set high intentions with good purpose, humility, organization, and in coordination with others.

LINE 2: As a leader, be with and stay level to the team. Simultaneously stay connected to higher guidance. Pass rewards on to all who help. All goes well.

As a leader, I follow higher guidance, stay connected and level with followers, and share rewards.

LINE 3: Allow higher guidance to lead. At times this will come from others or other sources, and at times from within yourself.

I receive inspiration from higher guidance, within and without.

LINE 4: When overwhelmed, disengage with organized caution. Prepare for a better day.

I sense when respite is beneficial and take it.

LINE 5: With higher guidance, it is time for vigorous advance in an organized manner.

In this ripe time for inspired creativity, I proceed with organized enthusiasm.

LINE 6: It is a time of success. Sharing rewards multiplies them.

Sharing rewards multiplies them.

8. Unite in All Win

I unite in the manner that best serves each moment, following, leading, or co-creating.

 Open Space, Water
Receptive, Earth

Water flows over the earth, covering it with rivers, lakes, and oceans. When water comes together with more water, it merges with relative ease.

All lines in the hexagram are receptive except the fifth, which represents unity around a leader of high consciousness and intention. Know when to lead and when to follow. Being a leader is challenging. Explore your readiness to lead. If you are prepared to lead, proceed; if not, follow. Be flexible to shift from one to the other in each moment serving the whole well.

The best way to decide to lead or follow is to ask from which role you can serve the most. When you are ready to be a leader, your awareness will be focused upon the common good.

Timing is essential. If you arrive too late, you may miss out on things that would empower your serving.

A primary leading and uniting skill is listening well. To listen well, be sensitive to when another has a need to express and be heard deeply. A metaphor which helps this sensitivity is to notice when another has emotional force in their expression akin to water rushing from a container above to another below. Realize that as the upper container empties into the lower, there is little room for receptivity by the upper container until the upper container has emptied enough to have space to receive. During this emptying expression, listen with total silent presence within and without to the other.

Hold and release leadership harmoniously. When your highest priority is to serve, you intuit the best balance of taking charge and following. Shift fluidly between leader and follower to contribute the best in each moment. You will be blessed with success, fulfillment and joy.

LINE 1: Union is created by authenticity and kindness, not by mere words. Genuine love for humanity and each individual is the only thing that creates true union. This does not mean to support negative behavior; instead support the higher nature in everyone. Let those caught in lower nature go their own way. Spirit will unite with their dormant higher self and activate it. In the meantime, focus your energies upon uniting with those who manifest their higher nature. Seek out and relate to those with obvious purity in thought, words and deeds.

I connect in authentic kindness from and to higher nature.

LINE 2: Connect exclusively to the higher nature of others with self-respect and dignity. Never give up your self-esteem to another. Be reserved and hold back from others when they come from their lower nature and never give up on others reaching their higher nature. Spirit will correct them; you don't have to, you don't need to, and it is not your place or power to do so. Spirit will handle it. It helps for you to restrain coming from your lower nature. With this wisdom, know all is handled well; go your own way, and create a great life in union with those who manifest their higher consciousness.

I persevere in self-respect and dignity as I relate only with higher consciousness.

LINE 3: Preserve intimate relating for worthy things. Do not indulge negativity in yourself or others. Be reserved and observe appropriate timing in getting to know each other. Then unite only with that which is higher in each of you.

Moving slowly and carefully in the beginning, I come from and relate only to what's higher.

LINE 4: Be not embarrassed to be good, true, and loving. Authentic goodness ultimately bears exquisite and plentiful fruit. With those who manifest goodness, direct and open kindness is most effective. When others manifest a lower nature, outward reserve seasoned with inner blessing for their higher nature yet to be expressed furthers all.

I embrace and express pure goodness and await the same from others.

LINE 5: Do not try to hold others to you. Be your best self, and allow others to come and go as they please. Only connect where you have been welcomed or with issues you are invited to attend. Set your own healthy boundaries. Firmly hold back when you choose to remain private, and open where mutuality is natural and flows with grace, goodwill, and wisdom.

I am independent, yet gracious. I flow smoothly between my higher self and the higher self of others, leading, following, or co-creating the best each moment.

LINE 6: Whatever the task, whatever the challenge, to succeed takes holding together in harmony, within and with others for complete success.

I hold together with others in harmony throughout, and realize this is what total success requires.

9. SMALL STEPS REALIZE BIG DREAMS

*I take small gentle steps
which carry me to heavenly existence.*

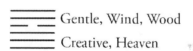 Gentle, Wind, Wood
Creative, Heaven

Heavenly creations are mastered in gentle steps. Move forward like a soft wind gently blowing only forward. Each moment, focus on one task only, letting go of all others until their moment arrives. You become absorbed. From this immersion, you conquer big challenges with less effort.

Let go of expectations for results into just doing good for the benefit of the whole. Transform worry about goals into savoring each creative step toward those goals. One day soon, you will come out of the ecstatic trance of presence, look up and see that which you have created is completed excellently. You will amaze yourself with the beauty, utility, and prosperity that you have created. A warm glow of fulfillment will make you wish you had created what you behold and in the next moment you will realize with joy that you did.

Mastery comes as you become lost in creating. This opportunity is yours now.

Be where you are. Sense what wants to be done. Pick a priority, or just jump in with the first thing at hand. Flow forward in steps that lead to completion, focused on the one step you are doing each moment, knowing all the while that you are living life well here and now. Flow forward with ease and grace, all the while basking in the excellence that spontaneously manifests in the process.

LINE 1: Don't push ahead forcefully. Take a single easy step with joy and excellence, and then another and another. You travel to your goal as though you are flying on wings. The quality of results and experience will be higher than if you push, worry, and crowd your time. Slower is faster, better, and filled with joy.

I proceed in excellent easy steps that create joyful, creative, successful journeys.

LINE 2: What, how, and when should I take action? Flow. Do not force. Taking the right steps at the right time creates success. Observe and follow others who succeed. Trust your intuition to guide each step.

I trust flow, wise intuition and follow excellent models each step of the way.

LINE 3: Pushing ahead too much when it seems a little extra push will break through barriers, leads to reversals. Remain gentle and carefully conscious. Allowing and letting go are more powerful than excessive trying to control. Return to equanimity and calm. All good comes at the best time.

I allow and let flow.

LINE 4: Given the challenging task of advising another who is contemplating violence, use the calm objective power of truth to slowly return them to neutral. Tactfully alternate rapt listening with wise reflection upon likely consequences.

When called upon to advise another away from violence, I begin with rapt attention to gain information and influence. With excellent attention to openings for input, I intersperse with wise reflection upon likely consequences that steer away from harmful outcomes.

LINE 5: You prosper when you live by wise principles. Sharing these principles expands their benefit.

I thrive as I learn, live, and share wisdom.

LINE 6: In sensitive situations, success is achieved through small gentle steps. It is especially important to avoid arrogance with accomplishments. What was gained will be lost. Humility retains gains.

I gain heaven with humble cautious steps.

10. CAUTIOUS CONDUCT

*I create heavenly joy
with cautious conduct.*

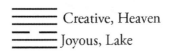 Creative, Heaven
Joyous, Lake

The joyous lake under the creative heaven calls for care in powerful circumstances. With care, heaven is attained. Herein lies wisdom in relating to power. The image is of treading lightly on the tail of a tiger. The tiger is powerful, and could turn and bite if the treading is heavy. On the other hand, because there is so much power, when it is handled well with caution, great achievements can be made. Cautious conduct brings good and prevents harm.

There is joy in care. A skilled carpenter uses tools to craft beautiful and useful wooden objects. The tools are sharp and would be dangerous if handled carelessly. With care, however, power yields joy in creativity.

Everyone has power in relationships. Creative joy brings heavenly results. Care and skill in all relationships bring excellent results and good emotions. Subtlety is of the essence. Good manners, softness, and tact create quality and success. Considerate lightness generates excellence with safety. The greater force treats the lesser gently. There is opportunity for one of lesser power to excel.

Skilled creativity begins in the heart. The heart informs the mind. Discern each thought you think. Thinking validates itself, so whatever perspective you take expands. Choose each thought with care as you would in finding secure footholds each step in climbing a sheer cliff. You avoid slipping and falling in a potentially dangerous environment that is otherwise beautiful and exciting.

Cocreate with the light. Be good to yourself and others. Stick to the higher and lighter side. Being good to others is being good to yourself. Respect others' interests in honoring conversation. Be sensitive to different roles. Find and validate the best in others. By creating common meaning and sharing benefits, you create the best in relationships, circumstances, and yourself.

Congratulations, you are empowered to realize dawning opportunities. Caution informs and transforms opportunities into heavenly reality.

LINE 1: Do what you do for the love of creating while allowing progress at its own pace. When one has achieved something, pushing for external advantage leads to arrogance and laziness. Gains are lost. Ego issues resolve when your sole intention is to contribute. To avoid such loss, love the act of creating worthy ends for themselves alone. This nourishes and fulfills you.

I love the act of creating for itself alone independent of ego.

LINE 2: To remain disentangled be non-confrontational, avoid inner conflict between what you wish were true and what is true by accepting what is and building from there. From this realistic foundation, you stay whole, calm, and succeed.

I remain calm and non-confrontational embracing life as it is, and proceed from here.

LINE 3: Focus upon the good and the pure in your heart. Let go of all else. Spirit will correct others if needed. Spirit is better equipped to do the job and handle the reactions. It serves the good of others to experience the consequences of their actions. Enjoy the harmony and peace of mind of limiting yourself to what's good.

I focus on the pure and good and let natural consequences carry the rest.

LINE 4: Proceed, but with extreme caution. Move forward gently with awareness. Offend no one. You retain freedom and accomplish your goals.

I proceed with extreme caution.

LINE 5: Caution and wisdom resolve danger. Inner wisdom guides you well. The *I Ching* is available to coach you along the way. You gain in the process.

I resolve danger with cautious wisdom in consultation with wise resources.

LINE 6: Your actions determine your success and joy. Keep doing what goes well and evolving what does not.

I persevere in what goes well and allow the rest to evolve.

11. Peace

*I receptively
co-create expanding peace.*

 Receptive, Earth
Creative, Heaven

The two essential energies of life, the creative and the receptive, move together bringing peace. Active creative energy below moves upward toward the receptive; earth above moves downward toward the creative, heaven. Being receptive to heavenly creative forces manifests heavenly experience.

As you tune in to what is highest and best for all concerned, including yourself, you create profound paradise. In peaceful balance, move forward carefully considering the best place and pace to proceed.

Receive inspiration from completions already achieved; envision what you want most to create and proceed with the single best next step. You experience joyously creating heavenly existence. Seeing things that are already accomplished fills you with confidence to go the rest of the way in fulfilling dreams. Creatively using that joyful energy helps fulfill those dreams. Proceeding in harmony with others and circumstances brings about excellence.

All things change. Accepting change generates good times returning sooner and remaining longer. Gratitude for peaceful presence expands blessedness. Practice joyful presence and proceed. Include others in your goodwill and good fortune. The love and joy you generate, returns to you.

LINE 1: All aspects are aligned. Action accumulates success after success. Keep going. Keep growing. Stay positive, humble, and healthy. Progress is assured when you share your good fortune.

All goes well as I persevere in humility, generosity, and positive action.

LINE 2: In times of personal peace and prosperity, keep creating with generous kindness. Be open to and accept others who may not be experiencing similar serenity.

I accept and nurture others who may not now be experiencing similar serenity.

LINE 3: Tranquility and progress increase and decrease. Steadiness when there is decrease hastens and ensures increase. Your general happiness rises with more elevated lows and highs.

I elevate down's and up's, raising both.

LINE 4: Seek not to change others. Be neutral, natural, and unhurried. Then peace permeates all.

I produce peace through accepting others as they are.

LINE 5: Serenity abounds as one serves others, the good, and the whole.

My serenity blossoms in the soil of my serving the good of the whole.

LINE 6: Accepting change is the first step in finding peace. Change is a constant in life. Be prepared for challenges. Set expectations accordingly. Rise to challenges. Accept them when they come. Peace returns.

I change things for the better by choosing change.

12. Being Still

My allowing reverses resistance.

 Creative, Heaven
Receptive, Earth

Be receptive to the creative. Realize the opportunity to stay still while conditions shift. Since heaven and earth move away from each other, it is a good time to nurture yourself by just allowing for the time being. Under such conditions, forcing can create resistance where allowing brings change for the better. You are nurtured now because less effort is required of you. Stay whole within as you allow without.

An essential principle of the *I Ching* is that change is constant. Present difficulties resolve on their own when accepted with gentle kindness. Support progress at this time by being particularly careful and caring.

Quiet inner focus helps now. The more you let go without and connect to your higher nature within, the better; even withdraw a bit when things don't go well. Avoid putting your ego above your higher self. Allow yourself to slow down, all the way to stillness. Go inside. Be still. Allow inner wisdom to guide you.

As challenges pass and you allow them to pass, you create good feelings about yourself and bless your reality. Those who meet challenge well, persevering in the best for all concerned, prove and improve themselves.

LINE 1: Persevere in stillness. When you meet resistance, disengage quietly. Others will do the same. All will be well.

As I peacefully disengage, others do likewise.

LINE 2: Small successes are better than big failures. Frustration, exhaustion, and challenges tempt negativity. These are opportunities to discover your worth. Energize your higher self. Disengage lower states. Put problems behind you. Find your center.

From this whole place, take on a small bit of the challenge you're facing. You are sure to succeed. You will stay balanced and joyful. Proceeding little by little, you handle challenges well, and you experience yourself as wise, kind, and happy. At this time, pay little heed to flattery from within or without which may entice you to overstep yourself.

I realize it is better to hold back now than push ahead prematurely, so I hold back.

LINE 3: Hold firm to goodness while allowing others to find their way. Those who are mistaken, when left to contemplate and self-correct, eventually realize the mistake from the natural consequences of their actions. For your part, take care to be good yourself. Withdraw from wickedness wherever it exists. Things improve everywhere.

As I immerse myself in the positive, the negative evaporates.

LINE 4: When led by goodness, you never fail. As you follow good, everything improves.

As I follow good, everything improves.

LINE 5: Positive change is at hand. By remaining faithful to wisdom and goodness, you help it along. Alter your path when necessary to conform to what's good, right, and true.

Embracing the good contributes to a better situation.

LINE 6: Be guided by good within. Follow your inner light. How? Reverently align with sacred sensing. Quiet your mind. Identify with Spirit, with pure being.

I follow good within.

13. Reverent Fellowship

In joyous deeply respectful fellowship,
I participate in cocreating
heaven on earth.

 Creative, Heaven
Connecting, Fire

Following your passion creates heavenly experience and existence. The fires of trust, goodwill, and creative genius burning in everyone unite inspiring cocreation of heaven on earth. Harmonize your passions with others. Experience the many flames dancing together bringing heavenly joy.

With modest honoring, hold back when appropriate. Allow space for big and small contributions and validations to be given and received from and to all.

Fan the flames of joyous exchange. Sense and support the best for everyone. Radiate light to everyone. See all people as a central sun in their own universe. Bring warmth to all. The more all souls are nurtured, the more each soul is nurtured. Play your part. Neither over nor under do it. Be with each other in gracious presence.

Flowing together in generous spirit adds mutual wealth of caring, trust, respect, and empowerment. Embrace simple, yet profound sources of mutual support. Today's simple social gatherings are tomorrow's communities of common benefit and mutual aid in emergency.

Come together frequently in friendly greeting. Gather round good purpose. Benefit each one. Your world becomes heavenly. Your heart sings with joy. As you hold gentle simple love of each human being, life manifests mutual caring and abundant friendship.

Flow in friendly fellowship with those of common interests, values, and preferences. Where there is less commonality, maintain healthy space and boundaries keeping friendly relations at appropriate distances. In healthy flexibility, allow these distances to wax and wane over time and with circumstances. Vary the distance needed for safe space or connecting by sensitively harmonizing your own and others' needs and desires.

Even though you may not be drawn into close fellowship with everyone at all times, maintaining good relations with each person is utterly valuable, and promotes your own and all others' best interests.

LINE 1: To begin well, listen well. Then express clearly. Hidden agendas, secrecy, or failing to listen to others, or expressing yourself clearly undermine good connections. Great relationships come from balancing authentic goodwill with openness, responsibilities, and rewards.

I balance listening first, then expressing clearly with love in exquisite harmony with others.

LINE 2: Include everyone in your goodwill and high intentions. Be aware of your preferences in style and values. Maintain mutual goodwill with healthy space and boundaries. Create neither prejudice nor factions against anyone. In the meantime, go your own way. Proceed in harmony with all that is good.

With goodwill for all, while varying wise social distance with each, I am inclusive.

LINE 3: Create an atmosphere of trust, openness and joy where people are welcomed, celebrated, and their good ideas and purposes are supported.

I create positive relationships of trust, openness, and joy, in welcoming support and celebration of others' good ideas and purposes.

LINE 4: It is better to create distance and space than to fight. With the peace created by sufficient personal space, issues resolve spontaneously. Resolve outer conflicts within. Have goodwill for yourself and others as resolution proceeds at a proper pace. Know your goodness as you proceed.

I give relationships healthy space.

LINE 5: As you treat others, so you treat yourself. Whatever occurs outwardly, inwardly let your higher self unite in friendship and harmony with the higher selves of all others. All things become better forever.

I permanently improve with every increasing generosity of spirit, for as I treat others I treat myself.

LINE 6: You are on the path of sacred union. Keep going. You are doing well.

I am on the path of nurturing relationships into sacred unions.

14. Abundant Treasures

The greatest gift I give myself
is giving to others.

 Connecting, Fire
Creative, Heaven

You create heavenly existence for yourself and others by passionately clinging to what is good, beautiful, and true. Great rewards and riches flow to and from you as you move forward with modest ease.

You are challenged to expand your capacity to receive; keep this flow coming to you by giving. Being generous and releasing your gifts support you to keep the flow open. Ever greater good comes to you and from you in a cycle of abundant giving and receiving.

Sharing creates relationships of joy and mutual blessing. There is no greater gift you can give yourself than giving to others. You nurture your own soul.

A far greater gift than material things is generous presence, characterized by goodwill with kind and uplifting attention to how others feel about themselves. To thus validate others, learn from them those good things they hold most dear and support these things.

Create a spirit of goodwill, joy, and confidence. Generate abundance for all in mutual giving and receiving. Be generous in your giving, and in your receiving. Allowing others to give to you honors them. Gently, respectfully acknowledge the gifts others are to you in their presence. How? With sensitive balance, let your eyes light up as you relate to those who like your attention, while giving space to those who prefer privacy. This varies over time with different people. You validate yourself and others by confirming the goodness within each of you. This kindness propels you forward in all your projects, dramas, and dreams. You are planting seeds of success on all levels when you allow yourself the pleasure and prosperity of validating all people, including yourself.

Enjoy abundance in relations with all others. With those who would take unfair advantage of such openness, discern and wisely hold back until they transform. With space and respectful treatment, they will evolve.

Have you ever envied people who seem to be ultimately happy, serene, and prosperous? You have the opportunity now to possess what you have envied. The source comes from your heart, from love. To unlock these treasures, ask *how can I make things better for other people and myself, not just for myself alone?* Let answers come. Fulfill the answers.

Observe precious gems of experience filling your soul. Many moments will fill your memory with precious people and richness of Spirit that is nothing less than a life well lived. You become more precious to yourself; knowing yourself as one of great heart and generosity, you become a living treasure to yourself.

As you build abundant being, you shine all the brighter. Your aura becomes a beacon appreciated by all. Because you are a vital part of life, your generous participation adds to the ever expanding wisdom of nature. Gently savor varieties of experience, every person, place, and essence in your presence.

Spirit brought you forth to be part of an abundant universe. Like all others, you are life. Enjoy your existence with gratitude, humility, and generosity. Reap a nourishing harvest. Allow the same for all others. Life is happening here and now. Don't miss it.

LINE 1: Know that as you begin, you will be challenged. Let go of expectations and love the learning. Give the gift to others of valuing yourself. Keep shifting challenges with wisdom. First, dissolve fear by continuing to evolve spiritually into what you know is good, excellent, and whole.

I love learning and therefore embrace challenges.

LINE 2: In calm goodness, share insights, skills and talents on a firm foundation of what's beautiful, good and true.

I give my gifts from goodness and wisdom.

LINE 3: Release ego-oriented self-praise in favor of Spirit-centered support of others. In this way, the gifts you give yourself are greater than the gifts you request. Your humble graciousness wins love, cooperation, and support. You experience bliss, blessings, wholeness, happiness, success, and fulfillment on all levels.

Unselfish giving is the greatest gift I give myself.

LINE 4: Look straight ahead on your own path. Neither compare nor boast of your possessions. Be true to yourself, your mission, your calling. Fulfillment arises from being the independent, unique you. Support success and prosperity for all.

With humility, joy, and independence, I give my unique gifts to others.

LINE 5: Pursue not the praise and appreciation of others. Give attention, support, respect, goodwill, and honoring by simple steps that most support what's best for others. The same returns to you.

I give with no thought of receiving, which paradoxically receives the most, for in giving I receive the most.

LINE 6: One prospers who is true, good, and humble. Being your highest, best self brings reward in all parts of life. You reach the height of existence.

Through humble goodness, I reach higher existence.

15. Reverent Humility

*I live in the sacred consciousness
of reverent humility.*

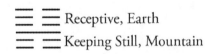 Receptive, Earth
Keeping Still, Mountain

Quiet your mind with the strength of a gentle mountain and the receptive nurturing of the entire earth. Into this vast openness, be as receptive as the earth for inner guidance. Embrace higher consciousness in your heart. With higher consciousness, your intention and intuition blossom.

Receive inner nurturing. Empty your consciousness of its cravings and ravings, replacing it with the open emptiness of the field of all positive possibility. How? Suspension, detachment, non-expectation. Suspension of what? Of the small frightened self. What good will suspension, nonattachment, and non-expectation do me? You will only get everything you ever wanted.

In this place of no ego separating you from ultimate good, things flow easily, naturally, and spontaneously. You will be surprised things go so well. You see things for what they truly are. You transcend your small self from the unreal to the real, from the mundane to the sacred, from partial alignment to wholeness, from lost and alone to loving and beloved. Alone transforms into all one.

Being one with all, your small, selfish, and scared goals transform into goals for the good of the whole. Scared becomes sacred. You radiate goodwill, caring, and carefulness. All beings immediately sense your benevolence and know you are a safe presence. Feeling safe with you, their hearts open spontaneously and welcome you. With hearts opened, the beauty of each of you becomes immediately transparent. Inward smiles of recognition dawn between you. You know each other's souls as the same in your divine human essence. Outpourings of loving grace envelope each other.

From this safe nonjudgmental openheartedness, feelings of love, validation, acceptance, and mutual compassion light your relationships. To judge is human; to see with compassion, divine. You never meet anyone you do not like. With your feet planted solidly on the ground, your heart, your soul lives in heaven. This blessedness brings health, happiness, and wholeness.

The cost of inner peace is keeping the mind still, present, and open. The quiet present mind is richer. The quiet present mind is fertile. The quiet present mind is healthy and holy. This is the consciousness in which the voice of Spirit can be clearly heard. Being empty and receptive, you arrive at cosmic consciousness. Welcome; you may stay as long as you remain open. You are embraced by light and love. You dwell in peace and wholeness. With humility, the perfection of imperfection is that each time you stray, with openness, even to your own missteps, you return wiser and still more whole.

LINE 1: As you achieve increasing levels of modesty, be modest, even about modesty. The best path is simple and straightforward. To get from where you are to where you want to be, proceed without expectation or disappointment, without self-importance or resentment at not being acknowledged. All dreams come true when pursued in humble focused excellence.

I am modest about being modest.

LINE 2: Others intuitively discern feigned modesty. Heartfelt humility expresses itself in all you embody attracting the greatest good to you.

Only authentic modesty truly connects. I find this within and live it.

LINE 3: Through modesty and approaching good, you may achieve recognition, even fame. If you swell in self-congratulation, you lose the recognition and the progress. If you remain humble and hold yourself with, not above, others, you are loved. Your successes, genuine contributions, and being appreciated continue to grow. Genuine modesty is an ingredient in total success without which success does not happen.

I am authentically modest, and only this succeeds.

LINE 4: Modesty brings success in both the low and the high. As a leader, honor and treat others with dignity and respect. As a follower, do the same, including yourself, in this treatment. In both roles, giving more is modest rather than doing little and pretending that is modest. Express and give your gifts. Follow your calling. Such true modesty brings true success.

I act in accord with knowing true modesty honors, respects, and contributes.

LINE 5: You are being modest by taking effective responsibility for yourself. Although modesty requires restraining arrogance, it does not mean allowing anything to happen in a weak manner. It is good to require others to treat you with dignity and respect by gently withdrawing if they do not. Likewise, in objective, inoffensive ways, taking strong action, being the strongest creative power in your own life, is appropriately modest. It is modest because you forego the arrogance of thinking you are so important that others should take care of you.

In true modesty, I take care of myself.

LINE 6: Failing to stand up for yourself is not modesty. This easy arrogance blames others, takes offense, and feels self-pity. Real modesty disarmingly corrects mistakes made about your intentions when you are seen in error. Appropriately standing up for yourself in an authentically humble manner that forgoes the temptation to counterpunch, yet lets the power of self-evident truth speak for itself, elevates consciousness for all.

Carefully remain free of giving offense by not taking offense, and thus avert escalating hostilities. True modesty well delivered in appropriate timing and amount has the beneficial effect of bringing the other to empathic compassionate understanding of what is true for you without being offensive. This disarms hostilities, increasing peace, harmony, and goodwill. The test of true modesty is to require of yourself that the above results will assuredly accrue from your actions before you take them.

I avoid taking offense by modestly letting the truth speak for itself. With compassion, wisdom, and modesty, I calm troubled waters.

16. Joyful Enthusiasm

I flow with sacred joy.

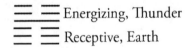
Energizing, Thunder
Receptive, Earth

Combine being as receptive as the earth with the energy of thunder. Be open and receptive to conditions, sensing the will and wants of those about you, and your own, all within the spiritual context of what wants to emerge. Sometimes this takes time and calm inner contemplation to discern well. Authentically find enthusiasm within to support what's better for all. Thus great rewards come with ease.

Following the path of greater gain and more flow is a core principle of the *I Ching*. This approach creates more with less. Creating more with less yields excellence, joy, satisfaction, and wholeness. Tune in to what is good, beautiful, and true, to what serves and supports everyone, including you. You manifest a delicious destiny with extraordinary ease and unparalleled excellence.

Proceed with delight in caring and care for your own and others' benefit. Become immersed in the stream of life. Enjoy the journey to treasures unknown. Possess jewels of joy, happiness and fulfillment.

Unfetter yourself. You are most true to yourself when you continuously disconnect from negativity. Any thought, word, or deed that invalidates you or another is off course. Keep pulling your awareness back to the path of what improves you, what feels better, what is pure and good. You are in the garden of grace when you fulfill your destiny to contribute, grow, nourish, and cherish all things and people.

Especially nurture your own sacred self, unselfishly. Manifest your higher nature, that which is noble within you. In such moments, you are deeply connected to Source. Connection is everywhere and always available. Just choose it.

LINE 1: Enthusiasm that boasts brings downfall. Only display enthusiasm that joins hearts.

I am humble in my enthusiasm.

LINE 2: Have fun, yet be aware of where any direction will take you. Correct early if headed the wrong way. Remain harmonious, whole, calm, and centered. To sacrifice is to make sacred. Keep coming back to silence within, to joy, to peace, to harmony and goodwill. Ecstasy is the reward.

I enjoy with care.

LINE 3: Be self-directed. To waver creates instability. Find good in each moment. Stick to it. Benefit all concerned. Keep disengaging from negativity. Create your own path, one aligned with higher consciousness, with what serves others and you.

I persevere in self-directed joy for all concerned.

LINE 4: The most enthusiastic support comes to those who share this enthusiasm from their deepest heart. Sense and seek what's better for everyone concerned. Without end, keep returning to all win. The resultant bliss supports you endlessly. *Love is a discipline of joy.*[4]

I let go of false enthusiasm and embrace only authentic enthusiasm with boundless joy for all beings.

LINE 5: False enthusiasm has no proper place. If one is genuinely not feeling enthusiasm, it is a drain to pretend. Authentic acceptance of one's true emotional state creates deeper connection with one's own soul and true healing. Healthy awareness and healing come from being true to yourself while giving competent empathy to others.

I embrace enthusiasm that heals and is charged with acceptance of self and others.

LINE 6: Enthusiasm for new nurturing brings joy. Enthusiasm for that which is ultimately harmful to self or others does not. Embracing enthusiasm that only nurtures creates great good.

I embrace enthusiasm that only nurtures and creates great good.

17. The Serving Leader

I joyfully follow
those I would lead.

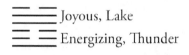Joyous, Lake
Energizing, Thunder

Thunder energizes oceanic joy. You have great influence now; use it well. Thunder awakens you to spreading joy as across a vast lake by serving those who would follow you as equals in co-creation of heaven on earth.

Stay true to the divine within. Consider others' ideas, plans, and strategies. Inspire them toward the best for all concerned. Joyfully co-vision and co-create in high mindedness.

Spread goodwill. Embrace a variety of viewpoints. Hone inner connection and harmonize self with the jewels of others'. Generate inner joy by holding to what you know to be good and true. Journey together from visions to dreams coming true. Welcome to heaven on earth. This is the joy you came to experience, the gifts you came to give, the life you came to love.

Like a lake fed by wellsprings of wisdom, goodness, and grace, bliss and fulfillment grow from joyful expression and contribution. Every loving thought, word, and action adds another drop of joy.

Follow the inner light for constant improvement. With self-evolution and contribution to others, everything around you improves. Participate fully, enthusiastically, and wisely in life, and those things you can do each moment to better yourself and the lives of those near and far. Subtle and self-evident rewards overflow for you.

As you serve those who would follow, let them tell you what they think and value. Be open and unattached. Blend with the work, wisdom, and wholeness of others. You will be as a joyous child playing in a lake on a summer day. In this stance, you advance the divine work of benevolent substance.

You lift up your life, love, and longevity through following sacred Source as the primary cause in all you do. Only good comes from this.

As circumstances, relationships and opportunities arise, shift to ever-higher levels of existence. Fear not; all is unfolding for the greater good. As you lead and follow, fill your heart with real joy. Embrace joy beyond what you've ever known or dared dream. For joy is the focal point of love.

Congratulations, you are connected to Source. Center your attention on this connection. Keep coming back to its purity. Your soul is continually refreshed and renewed. You know you are following the right path each moment you touch authentic joy.

LINE 1: It is time to influence the world. Listen with respect to others' concerns and values. Draw wisdom from all variety of sources, not only those who share your opinions. You co-create great good.

I give and receive that which is of highest value from all variety of sources.

LINE 2: The greatest single influence in one's life is the nature of one's relationships. Relate from your higher self and let go of the rest.

Relating from my higher self elicits response from others' higher self. I relate from higher self to higher self.

LINE 3: Evolve those lower things that once may have pleased you. Release them. Make room for the higher.

I evolve by releasing the lower for the higher.

LINE 4: A degree of success attracts followers. Some would flatter and manipulate. Others are authentically motivated for good. Free yourself from the former by letting go of vanity. Joining with others for common good fulfills you.

I forego flattery and simply favor being, doing, and relating to the good.

LINE 5: There is nothing truer to self than being true to what's beautiful, good, and true, particularly when inclined to do the opposite. Such choices are the heartbeat of a good life.

I know and practice true self-interest; this is true goodness

LINE 6: Releasing personal pressure, yet returning to assist others generates, lasting goodwill. One may have found inner peace and personal freedom through perseverance in self-evolution. Then another may come along seeking assistance. Returning to the world of effort to assist the one seeking help, a deep mutual bond is created. In giving such assistance, stay true to higher nature.

I make the best use of my freedom by giving and staying true to higher guidance.

18. Refresh, Renew

*I refresh, rejuvenate,
and repair inside and out.*

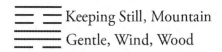 Keeping Still, Mountain
Gentle, Wind, Wood

Like a gentle breeze clearing the air at the base of a quiet mountain, fix up, clean up, repair, make amends, and renew. Steady gentle winds below clear out and freshen your foundations.

A profound, yet subtle, new energy eases your way. Renewal is in the air. Rare opportunities are abundant to improve your physical, personal, and social circumstances. Set your sails; cruise with the breeze. Release the old. Welcome the new.

Sense and express a new wind carrying you to fresh joy. All things, people, and a new spirit within compel, comfort, and assist you to clean up and complete with easy excellence. What were once daunting tasks are now a breeze.

Time and energy are available to you now with opportunity that will pass you by if you do not act soon. Would you rather leave things undone and dragging you down, or experience completions lifting you up?

Opportunity knocks. You will find flow and fulfillment tackling tasks that were once put off for the right day. This is that day. You are the one.

LINE 1: Following detours keeps you stuck. Don't miss out. With new attitudes and avenues, adapt and advance.

I adapt, advance, and avoid detours with new attitudes and actions.

LINE 2: Shift from stuck to soaring. Go easy; all flows well. Harshness and judgment slow your progress. Present focus, neither past nor future smoothes the way. Enjoy life while you're focusing in the present.

I shift from stuck to soaring by releasing negativity about the past and future and flow in the present with ease, excellence, grace, and joy.

LINE 3: Correct mistakes. Assign no blame. Simply proceed firmly forward in faith that all will be well and it will.

I correct mistakes assigning no blame and proceed knowing all will be well.

LINE 4: Contemplate creative ideas that shift things. Sticking to outmoded means slows you down. Stay on the path of progress and what comes naturally. Acting with compassion, kindness, and creativity yields high quality experiences and results.

I explore creative new ideas with compassion and kindness that expand my life.

LINE 5: Know you will succeed and you will. Accept assistance of helpful inner guidance, people, and circumstances. Shift as needed to complete things.

I know I will succeed as I avail myself of excellent assistance and flexibly shift as needed to complete things.

LINE 6: It is all right for one who seeks wisdom to withdraw into solitude. Letting go of day-to-day affairs empowers contemplation. To advance great works that bring profound benefit, it is valid to create time and space to support the effort.

I validate inward focus to evolve great works and wisdom.

19. Careful Caring Approach

I approach with highest intentions.

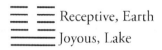 Receptive, Earth
Joyous, Lake

As you approach higher consciousness, joy grows within, like a lake covering the land. As pure water fills a spring-fed lake from within and rivers and streams fill a lake from without, fill yourself from within and without with joy and good. Savoring the pure fills you with joy.

With wisdom, joy expands. Approach wise counsel within and without. Within, open your heart, mind, and will to higher Source. Without, seek guidance from wise, high consciousness friends, mentors, and other resources. Sacred sources like the *I Ching* bring wisdom from both within and without.

Be as receptive as the earth to the highest. The most influential thing in life is the consciousness you nurture. You nourish your consciousness most by the relationships and thoughts you cultivate. Be receptive to the best influences and gently let the rest go.

To set healthy inner boundaries with lower thoughts, simply say to that part of you, *thank you for your opinion,* and move back to more constructive perspectives. You may find that this clears up lower levels quickly or over time. Or you may find value in other approaches, such as further *I Ching* readings or consulting wise friends or mentors, or meditating. Find a way to explore, then embrace new, higher ways of being and doing.

Gently, yet effectively, set healthy boundaries on the outer level with tactful words and phrases like:

- ○ *Let me think about it.*
- ○ *I'll get back to you if this seems like the best course of action for me.*
- ○ *Thank you for offering. I'm afraid that won't work for me right now.*
- ○ *I'm afraid I have a prior commitment I must honor.*
- ○ *I can't guarantee anything. Perhaps you'd best keep your present position or pursue other options.*

With freedom firmly established with healthy limits, you are empowered to approach opportunities that ring true with an open heart. You benefit by gentle and careful cultivation of humility, slowly taking time to assess the situation while persevering steadily ahead. Accumulating myriad good things creates delightful details in the doing, results, and sharing.

With due caution, approach the best in life and watch it bloom. Don't be afraid to ask for and receive the best assistance.

Begin within. Connect to higher purposes, to the beautiful, good, and true in you. Proceed slowly. Radiate goodwill. Proceed in the light of love.

Congratulations, great things are readily available to you now as you approach higher ways: slowly, humbly, heartily with excellent timing, sensing the best moment to act or hold back. Doing just the right amount of the right thing at the right time creates great goodness.

LINE 1: Going forward as a team, coordinated in agreement on goals and means brings success. Avoid rushing ahead. As success comes, stay calm and balanced; make decisions carefully. Excess excitement at the beginning from successes that come early can throw you off course. Equilibrium requires equanimity. Staying balanced, you succeed.

I go forward with others as a team, remaining calm and balanced with early successes and thus the successes continue.

LINE 2: All goes well with high intentions even with up and down cycles. As long as you follow higher purpose, you succeed.

I follow higher intentions knowing they sustain success.

LINE 3: When things go well, you may be tempted to carelessness; this invites reversals. Remain reverent. Repair mistakes, forgive, clear your mind, and move on. You grow and succeed from it all.

In good times or challenging times, I persevere in the good. The good times are renewed and preserved.

LINE 4: You have achieved a position of influence. Remain open to giving and receiving wisdom and assistance. Benefiting others sustains your success.

Advance continues as I share and include others.

LINE 5: To achieve higher goals and sustain an elevated existence, attract helpers of high integrity and skill. Give them the freedom to proceed in ways they do best.

I attract helpers of high integrity and skill and give them the freedom to proceed in their own best ways.

LINE 6: Although you may have created a beautiful nest within, from time to time it may be valuable to come out of that nest. Doing so in goodwill graces you and all you touch.

As I emerge from my beautiful inner sanctuary to share, my state of grace grows

20. Contemplate and Transform

I contemplate and practice
higher principles.

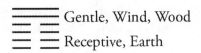 Gentle, Wind, Wood
Receptive, Earth

An ancient Chinese tower symbolized by this hexagram, calls forth higher nature standing as an example for all to see. Wind covering the earth bespeaks your expanding influence as you contemplate higher things and are seen as an example.

Thought directs energy. You become what you focus on. Contemplating universal laws like those in the *I Ching*, you become an example of the higher principles you ponder and live.

Higher consciousness includes awareness of what can be in the light of what is. You become wiser, seeing the truth of what is, what could be, and how to move from the one to the other.

This is a sacred moment in evolution, after new understanding, before change, with the wisdom and courage to make the journey safely and wisely.

In this time between awareness and action, set your path to be beautiful, good, and true, to be wise, kind, humble, and detached. Accepting leads you to increasingly higher existence, influence, and results. Embracing this wisdom within, you make the most of this precious journey.

LINE 1: With careful contemplation, all goes well. A position of responsibility and trust calls for deep understanding. Contemplation of what's right and good for all concerned is the foundation. Influence requires maturity and careful consideration of the whole.

To promote success, I carefully contemplate what is better for all concerned.

LINE 2: The broader your perspective, the wiser your choices. Integrating wisdom of others expands your own.

I invite and integrate others' wisdom.

LINE 3: Don't limit the basis of your decisions to externals and what others would do. As you contemplate possibilities, look to your values and listen to wisdom within. Make the ultimate criteria for choices be what you know to be good, beautiful, and true. You create excellence for all concerned.

I look deep within for right thought, choice, and action.

LINE 4: First, master self. Evolve your thoughts, motivations, goals, and actions. Align with what's higher. Seek purity. Go deep within. Touch the heart of your soul in peaceful contemplation. As your wisdom grows, so grows your influence. Be generous, yet humble, honoring, yet independent. Share wisdom gained in roles of influence and leadership. Your evolution is obvious to all about you.

First, I master myself.

LINE 5: As you evolve, your influence expands. Stay sensitive to what is beautiful, good, and true in each situation. Deep contemplation brings meaning and fulfillment. Foreseeing the effects of one's attitudes and actions, you remain whole and free of blame. Wisdom arises from careful consideration in calm reverence.

In calm reverence, I contemplate and manifest excellence.

LINE 6: Addressing the laws of nature and how they benefit the whole, you move beyond benefiting your life alone. Realizing how to remain innocent by sensing and doing what is beautiful, good, and true, you move beyond benefitting your life alone.

As I transcend contemplating only my life and address how the laws of nature affect the whole, I profoundly benefit the whole.

21. The Power of Choice

I discern, decide, act, and complete.

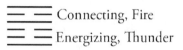 Connecting, Fire
Energizing, Thunder

The image: an open mouth with an obstruction in the middle, which one bites through. The trigrams thunder and fire suggest the thunder and lightning of a vigorous storm, which prescribe decisive action. Biting through the obstruction creates completion.

Carry out the completion in the right way. You have the power to choose what, where, when, and how to focus your attention and consequent actions. Continually return to your higher self. When inner obstacles appear, drop your doubt. Keep your consciousness clear to hear the quiet inner wisdom that will always guide you to the highest good.

When the obstacle comes from another, withdraw to the inner plane, yet relate outwardly with quiet respect. Natural consequences correct others. A balanced approach to others' transgressions, neither too severe nor too yielding, brings freedom. In your own actions, reconnect to higher principles.

Being free, while connected to higher consciousness, brings grace and wholeness. Feel this blessing. Connect to aliveness; open inner doors.

Like a fresh, safe, warm waterfall, allow life to wash over, cleanse, and free you.

With inner connection, wherever you are, you are safe at home within. Be present in and to the loving nurturance. Stay present and receptive to good for others and yourself. You create uninterrupted grace. Grace is here for you each moment you welcome it.

You radiate light and goodwill, healing and nurturing. You are welcomed and treated well everywhere. You bring benefits, intended and unintended. Your days, your life, your existence are filled with constant blessing as you continue biting through to right thought and action. Savor the wholeness and the blessings.

LINE 1: Do the right thing and all goes well. Learning from first mistakes prevents increasingly harsh consequences. Be mild in correcting others.

I do the right thing, learn from mistakes, and am mild in correcting others.

LINE 2: All turns out well if you avoid going too far correcting others. Remain outwardly modest and humble, yet inwardly firm. When necessary, move away from one who fails to treat you with dignity and respect.

I am outwardly humble while inwardly firm. I gently give myself space from the harshness of others.

LINE 3: Joy brings love. Lingering in blame and revenge poisons the mind and punishes the punisher. If issues arise, keep shifting back to joy and love. You will soar.

Letting go of revenge, which punishes the punisher, I shift to joy and love, which sets me soaring.

LINE 4: Reconnect with Spirit within. Outwardly, it is advisable to withdraw in a firm moderate way. Find the optimal path that is neither too hard nor too soft. You will succeed. In the meantime, let inner connection nurture you.

I firmly but gently free myself by withdrawing from harsh treatment while remaining deeply connected within.

LINE 5: You transcend danger and difficult situations unharmed and whole. Allow others to learn from experiencing the consequences of their actions. Ally only with others where you each independently intend what is right and good. Be aware of being too lenient or too harsh. Higher guidance leads you well.

I practice independent balanced self-regulation and thereby transcend circumstances unharmed and whole.

LINE 6: Seeing and correcting errors early brings joy. The sooner one returns to humble acceptance of right and good, the better the results. With one's own or other's errors or both, you are rewarded for awareness, discerning, and doing right. Consequences occur if you do not. Staying aware without and connected within brings joy.

I quickly discern and do right.

22. True Grace

*I explore and express
true grace from deep within.*

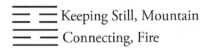 Keeping Still, Mountain
Connecting, Fire

Be like a calm mountain with molten fire deep within. Feel a fire within you of true passion for deep worth. Be in the world in gracious quiet harmony. Bring the authentic worth of who you are to what you do.

Surface attractions mean little if they are limited to externals. Bring forth your best from deep within. Be real, and just, and kind to all. Feel your heart's loving and wise guidance long and well before critical decisions and actions. Consider all viewpoints; integrate them into a balanced whole. Plan and act for the good of all concerned.

Know that everyone and everything has a sacred center. Accordingly, treat all others, yourself, and each thing you do and say with reverence. Honor and respect returns to its source.

Clarity for highest intentions protects and sets you free. Advance with sufficient slowness to know and do what truly is most honorable and honoring. Constant integrity keeps you connected, never alone, transforming alone to all one.[5]

Spirit blesses creations that advance Its good. Much benefit comes as you connect with and advance goodness with grace. Meditate on this knowing to keep your inner light glowing.

At your core, you are truly gracious. You are of deep worth to the world and to yourself. As you live and express yourself from this sacred center, you are trusted, loved, cherished, prospered, celebrated, and welcomed by others' open hearts and minds. As you treat the world, so you are treated. Contribute profound value, kindness, and joy.

Know: who I am, is what I do, and how I do it.

LINE 1: Especially in the beginning, leave luxury aside. Dig in and work hard with modesty and appreciation. You learn the essence of all things and earn the respect and goodwill of all.

My first step is to let go of luxury and work hard.

LINE 2: Do deeply important things first. Prioritize by values.

I do what I value most highly first.

LINE 3: With successes, do not stop. Keep progressing calmly and modestly.

With success I do not stop, I calmly proceed with modesty.

LINE 4: Choose simple over fancy. Humble purity fulfills far more than empty vanity.

I simplify.

LINE 5: You are authentically loved for who you are, not what you have. Let go of lust for wealth and show. Spirit most supports authentic goodwill, kindness, and love in action.

I express love simply in my being and actions.

LINE 6: Shift from surface to soul.

I choose substance over surface.

23. Free Yourself

I peacefully free myself without
and nourish myself within.

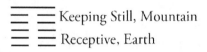Keeping Still, Mountain
Receptive, Earth

An old mountain rests serenely on the earth with the wholeness of independent self-assurance. It beautifies the landscape offending no one. Free yourself from externals; enjoy the inner life, which gives great space, and thereby abundantly blesses those about you and yourself.

Take on less. It is best to let things be for now. Disengage peacefully with goodwill. All will be well.

LINE 1: The best course of action now: turn back and wait for a better time.

I turn back and peacefully wait for a better time.

LINE 2: Seek assistance carefully. Keep replacing negative perspectives and conditions with positive.

I disengage the negative and engage the positive.

LINE 3: Disengage from negative relationships safely and quickly. Although others may desire something different, follow this best course. Connect with constructive people, your own higher nature, and inner wisdom.

I free myself to follow the good, wise, kind, and joyful.

LINE 4: Accepting challenges brings the best results.

For best results, I accept and embrace challenges.

LINE 5: In an instant, a whole school of fish can turn as one. So can you. Be bold. Hold to new enlightenment in every moment. People get the message; it is so visible. Your existence improves again and again, one instant after the other.

I shift to the positive immediately and totally.

LINE 6: Activating higher self, problems pass. Languishing in what is lower multiplies problems. Hard times transform to good ones with a shift in your attention. Make weathering adversity pay in wisdom gained.

I replace lower with higher and gain.

24. Good Times Return

You are blessed with benevolent new beginnings.

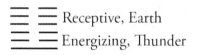 Receptive, Earth
Energizing, Thunder

New energy rises through the earth. A blade of grass sprouts into the light. Excellent conditions return. The spirit of springtime lights your life now.

The sun is rising in your life right now. Awaken slowly, stretch, and savor. Winter turns slowly to spring. Begin gently. Great growth, prosperity, and happiness dawn for you. Play your part with ease, love, and flow.

Little by little experience how increasing energy pulls you up. Enjoy. Weed negativity from your consciousness. There is no place, and blessedly no need, for fear in the higher self. An easy, quick, and effective way to remain in the higher self is to *hit the delete button* every time fear appears in your consciousness. Clear the fear by saying inwardly to yourself; *delete.*[6] Free yourself from past mistakes with increasingly constructive feelings, thoughts, and action.

It is a time to be optimistic. Things go well. And yet it is a time when new shoots grow best with tender treatment. Rather than push, allow. Ease things along with care.

Rain and sun provide good growing conditions, yet avoid too much of either. Be optimistic and optimal, not too much and not too little.

The natural result of carefully cultivating the best for all is creating the best life you can live.

LINE 1: Step out of destructive patterns before getting stuck there. Mistakes are inevitable; don't invalidate yourself for making them. Simply transform, transcend and move on. A powerful way to do this is to substitute positive perspectives for every negative one that comes up. Forgive yourself for false beliefs that you are less than love. You prosper from all things when you proceed in this manner.

I gain from mistakes by learning, changing, and moving on; and by forgiving myself for the false belief that I am less than love.

LINE 2: Let go of past burdens. Start fresh. Renew positive relations with self, others, and life.

I start fresh by releasing the past and proceeding with the new.

LINE 3: Allow the three senses of light: lighthearted, light-weighted, and illuminated. Persevere and inspire. Progress with a steady step, a loving hand, and a whole heart. Be certain of the good, the sacred, and the innocent. All these things will heal you. You will find your center, brighten your spirits, and feed your soul. Keep going; your best dreams are coming true.

I progress and heal with a steady step, a loving hand, and a whole heart embracing the good, the sacred, and the innocent.

LINE 4: Be independently connected to your higher self, to higher thoughts, feelings, actions and results.

I am independent, connected to my higher self, and to higher thoughts, feelings, and actions.

LINE 5: Life does not make you suffer; mistaken thoughts and beliefs that you are not okay do. You have the power to choose. Change negative patterns and your life changes. Repair. Clean up past mistakes within and without. Proceed with joy and harmony. You will succeed.

To succeed, I transform thoughts about who I am to be increasingly conscious and constructive.

LINE 6: Missing opportunities to know myself as pure love increases the time until rewards return. Immediate benefit comes from awakening to my essence as love.

Knowing I am love, I transform right now.

25. INNOCENT PRESENCE

I live, laugh, and love
in innocent present presence.

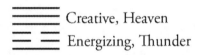 Creative, Heaven
Energizing, Thunder

Thunder energizes new heights of heavenly creativity as you live, work and just be in innocent present presence. Simply focusing upon each moment with highest intentions, without adding burdens, you arrive at goals spontaneously in joy.

The energizing thunder and the creative heaven, two powerful forces, combine opening the way for you now. Present moment focus with benevolent intentions brings excellent progress. What you intend and focus upon increases.

Enjoy childlike innocence with the wisdom of an elder.

Join with Spirit. Take each step with joy and care. You will flourish. Relish the process. It will be fun, creative and productive bringing inner and outer reward. Just as what you send out returns to you multiplied, as you give away joy, kindness, and love, these are now yours in abundance. With innocence, welcome to benevolent being.

LINE 1: You are guaranteed good when you are unattached and pure.

I live in the certainty that good arises when I am unattached and pure.

LINE 2: There is no other focus so safe, creative and fun as the present moment.

I live in the safety, flow, joy, and creativity of the present.

LINE 3: Loss and gain are created within. Ultimately, it's all about your connection to Source through the perspective you choose and the meaning you make. Reconnect to what's good. You return to innocent present presence, to the state of grace, to your higher self, to oneness with higher consciousness, infinite wisdom, wholeness, joy, creativity and love.

I live in the grace of purity and presence.

LINE 4: Live from the inside out rather than from the outside in. Follow good, wise, and pure, the essence of inner innocence. You will be fine and do well.

Live from the light within.

LINE 5: "A merry heart doeth good like a medicine . . ." (Proverbs 17:22). Choose, feel, and love a merry heart no matter what; you will be forever grateful you did and do.

I keep a merry heart.

LINE 6: Sometimes are good times to wait for the right time. This is one of those times.

I await the right moment in calm wholeness and clarity.

26. Create Heaven within Through Stillness

In keeping still,
I create heaven inside and out.

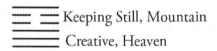 Keeping Still, Mountain
Creative, Heaven

Heaven is a state of mind. How do you create a heavenly state of mind? Your attitude and your thoughts create heavenly existence. Follow *the discipline of joy, the discipline of love.*[7] This is always available.

To create heaven inside and out, start by quieting the mind. Be like a mountain; not a tall jagged ego, rather an ancient, soft, rounded mountain, calm, whole, and anchored on the earth.

Create calm. It helps to know the nature of your brain and mind. Then use this knowledge. Neurons that fire together wire together. The more you practice being calm when things go well, the calmer you are in the midst of challenge.

When overstressed, rest until you are calm again. Do many calming activities like meditating, contemplating, resting before you are exhausted, listening to soothing music, or consulting inspiring people or inspired works, such as the *I Ching*. Practice being still.

Although meditation and contemplation are somewhat different, each facilitates and flows well into the other.

Meditate. Empty your mind as much as possible. For the rest, just watch thoughts come and let them go. Be aware of your breath. Focus quiet attention within on your being; simply put gentle loving attention on your gentle loving attention itself.

Contemplate. Be quietly aware of a specific subject. Watch with ease. You broaden and deepen your understanding.

From quiet centered contemplation, flow in and out of meditation. Watch your thoughts and the world go by. Stay focused on the beautiful, good, and true while transforming and letting the rest go.

Be aware of all you are and can be. This practice energizes self-determination, self-control, and self-discipline essential to creating self-realization.

To create dreams coming true, focus first on visions. Next, see pathways from here to there. Take small doable steps. Choose the best path and follow it observing optimum pace, rhythm, and rest. Enjoy the journey. Include positive rituals that ease the way.

Experience merging with your higher self. Start with visions and goals; chunking steps into optimal size and specifics to savor. Creating delicious visions and following them in joyful action is the essence of a fulfilling life. You progress in positive, forward, upward directions.

See the best you. Follow your Spirit upward. Cultivate and weed the garden toward your higher self. Thus, you create your own heavenly existence. Your relationships, your projects, and knowing your own goodness, your sacred self, become the truth of who you are, what you express, and how you live. Welcome to heaven.

LINE 1: Pause a moment. Hold back until the right moment to act, which is not quite yet. Ripe time will come soon. For now, do not push prematurely.

I wait for the right moment to begin.

LINE 2: Self-discipline builds moral fiber and creative power. Self-discipline means pushing forward and holding back with excellent timing, discernment, and rhythm. Now is a moment to hold back, build energy and allow circumstances to align. As you do, all goes well.

I *stop now and begin when timing is excellent. I await and allow circumstances to align and inform me what, how, and when to proceed.*

LINE 3: You may proceed now but be cautious. Move toward your goal. At the same time be safe. Develop yourself. Ally with what's good in all people and yourself, and all will go well.

I slowly and carefully begin.

LINE 4: Allow; don't push. Flow; don't force. One of the best ways to achieve and maintain equanimity is to set a smooth course. Envisioning things going well increases the likelihood they will. Stay on course. Being calm and whole, you will be more effective with less effort. Extreme good fortune is yours now.

I set myself on a smooth course.

LINE 5: Changing the nature of oneself and one's relationships re-channels potentially destructive events. Cultivating calm, quiet kindness inwardly and outwardly transforms potentially painful experiences into ecstatic ones.

I *shift to positive being and reap positive results.*

LINE 6: Congratulations, you have achieved heaven within. All your energy and power are now focused to bring success. You are creating heavenly existence for those near and distant, and for yourself.

Having achieved heaven within, all energy and power are now focused to bring success and fulfillment. Through connection to inner wisdom, I maintain momentum.

27. Soul Nurturing

I nourish myself and others deeply.

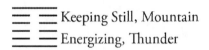Keeping Still, Mountain
Energizing, Thunder

Energizing thunder shifts to keeping still like a mountain. This inspires awakening and evolving. The hexagram as a whole suggests the open mouth of a parent bird feeding its baby. With its openness in the middle, the image suggested is nurturing others and yourself. Nurture yourself so that you may all the more nurture others.

Awaken your higher nature with all its enlightening, rejuvenating, joyous, giving, growing wisdom. Nurture yourself with the gift of an evolved self. Transform lower energies to higher ones. For example, transform the energy of anger or frustration into peaceful presence and subsequently carry out what's necessary for successful resolution. In the face of challenge, embrace harmony, peace, love, and all that is pure. The sacred manifests in you now, both for you, and in the gift you are to others.

Before you even let a thought, word, impulse, or action rest in your being, filter out all that could be destructive to you, others, or your relationships. Let all things in you be beautiful, good, and true. All your days will be filled with goodness, truth, and beauty. Proceeding on this path is a deep spiritual purification.

You have the opportunity to choose who you are. Who do you choose to be? To the world? To loved ones? To yourself? When challenges arise, would you like to be calm, whole, and competent? This is who, what, and how you can be now and in the future.

Know yourself as a truly good person, a soul who exquisitely cares for others and yourself. When your mission in life aligns with goodness, love, nurturing, and service, you are empowered. Beauty, being in the eye of the beholder, is that which inspires, uplifts, nurtures, and heals you. Find and follow your own pathway.

When you align with goodness, good envelopes you. You live in grace; your life blossoms in love and beauty.

You are life. Return to your natural nurturing center, to your higher self. This way you create dreams coming true. Continuing to keep your consciousness and conscience clear transforms visions into reality. Congratulations, you are on the path of wholeness, health and happiness.

LINE 1: Let a quiet open mind embrace higher possibilities. Know how valuable you are.

I let go of envy or doubt of others and know authentic self-worth.

LINE 2: Excessive dependence on others undermines self-esteem and personal power. Enjoy freedom and knowing true self-worth by giving more than you take. Stay connected to wisdom and joy within. Create and give. You will be free, whole and happy.

With self-reliance, I realize joyful freedom.

LINE 3: Heavenly existence awaits you. Immediate pleasures that create long-term pain and loss are false nourishment. You create the best possible existence when you embrace what nourishes others and your higher self over the short-, medium-, and long-term. Then, you are a gift to others and yourself. Your life has meaning, purpose, satisfaction, and fulfillment.

I create heavenly existence by giving attention to the long-, medium-, and short-term effects of my thoughts and actions.

LINE 4: Fulfilling great goals and intentions often require help. Obtaining such assistance requires limiting yourself to what is good, right, and true.

I strive to limit myself to constructive relationships. These relationships bring assistance when needed.

LINE 5: At present, you benefit from the support of one or more others. To keep such beneficial relationships whole and humming before taking on burdens of supporting others, wait and prepare until you are ready. Build inner strength and wisdom. Hold back until the time is ripe. Then move forward. All goes well.

I prepare well before supporting others.

LINE 6: As you evolve, you are increasingly able to care for others and yourself. Neither under nor over do it. Limits expand and contract over time. Be aware of their changing. Continue to grow, self-nourish and maintain wise limits. Be constantly receptive to inner knowing. Take on and release the right amount and you add to others and your own success and happiness.

I remain sensitive and responsive to my limits in the amount and nature of nurturing I attempt to give.

28. The Sweet Center

With much to do, I calmly optimize
taking exquisite care.
Great opportunities arise.

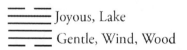 Joyous, Lake
Gentle, Wind, Wood

There is great opportunity now. Proceed humbly, yet joyfully, with the constancy of a gentle breeze blowing steadily in a single direction. With so much opportunity, there may be some pressure to overdo things. If handled well, with kindness, honoring, and respect for all, with moderation and mindfulness, each step moves things forward. Care feeds a lake of resources within you.

With so much to do when so much rides in the balance, think optimum rather than maximum. Treat everyone, including yourself, with exquisite respect. You are birthing great things. Proceed with refined gentleness and caution. Be generous of spirit, goodwill, and harmony with all. Express this harmony in every move and utterance.

You are creating great works. Balance just the right what, when, and how. With care and balance, you bring about conditions that realize your heart's visions.

Calmly envision opportunities being fully realized or on the path to their being so. Take your time. Enjoy the experience. Savor each step. Enjoy being alive, well, productive, and creative. Feel growth at nature's pace. You will cherish knowing you did well. You will enjoy yourself as you savor the doing. Let go of success until it spontaneously appears.

To generate energy essential for excellence, foresee the beauty and benevolence you are creating.

Allow Spirit's gentle hand to guide and embrace you. From this whole and healed place, allow the inner light to assist and teach you. A good way to receive Spirit's guidance is to clear your mind, focus inward, let go of past and future, and simply be present and quietly alert. You may even ask a question. Wait for the answer; it will come.

Spread Spirit's nurturance to all. Realize that this benevolent energy blesses you, everyone, and all things. Spirit's blessing is mirrored back to you as you shine it on others.

LINE 1: Begin great projects with gentle care and kindness. Proceed step-by-step.

I start big tasks gently.

LINE 2: Track Spirit's beam of gentle guidance. Be extremely careful with others so as not to break relationships so crucial in this time of heavy loads to be evenly, honorably, and respectfully distributed.

With deep inner guidance, I share the load with others evenly with respect and appreciation.

LINE 3: Pushing ahead too far, too fast creates breaking. Better go slowly with care and caution, allowing the right steps.

I savor slow excellence.

LINE 4: Others assist and things go well. But if one then holds the benefit only for one's self, more is lost than gained. It is meant for you to add to the whole. Then life adds to you.

I share the benefits with others.

LINE 5: Respect others' and your own strengths and limitations. As an elder and leader, bring wisdom and kindness to youthful energy. With youths' energy, assist elders and benefit from their wisdom. To transcend challenges, rather than going to extremes, bring out calm dedication in others, first by modeling. Co-create, while honoring others' wants and wisdom. Coordinate with inner gentle guidance.

I proceed honoring the wisdom of who is best to do specific tasks at any given moment.

LINE 6: Sometimes things go well, other times not so well. With either, when you pursue the good for its own sake, you do the right thing. The most precious possession of all, inner peace, is yours.

I follow good for its own sake and inner peace follows me.

29. Flow Like Water

*I flow joyfully
from wholeness to wholeness.*

 Open Space, Water
Open Space, Water

Water forms its shape effortlessly filling whatever surrounds it. It flows downhill. So too the best thing for you to do now is to flow with ease with whatever is. Fill each moment gracefully and graciously adapting to what is with ease. You arrive at your destination complete and fulfilled having avoided troubles.

Now is a time of change. Old ways may be replaced with new adaptations to abundant opportunities before you.

Embrace the new. Enjoy it. Lighten up in all senses of the word, heartfully, weightfully, and luminously. Shake off old patterns that may once have served you but now do not. Feel the vibrant life-giving quality of fresh pure water flowing through every cell. With no holding on, allow the old to go, lightening and brightening you.

Give yourself and all around you the gift of a vibrant you, yesterday older, today younger, wiser, and happier. When you flow with life, its joys await you. Wash your consciousness of any rigidity that would only hold you back.

Bask in an image of flowing fresh water. Wash yourself free of worry. Picture yourself beneath a gentle, natural hot springs waterfall. See it, feel it massaging out all stress. Let the visions carry all woes and worries downstream dissolving forever in an immense ocean of love.

Embrace challenges as opportunities and you make them precisely that. The greater the challenge, the greater the opportunity. You are on the verge of great things, of realizing your fondest dreams. You make opportunity real when you flow with events, people, and unexpected circumstances with acceptance and perseverance in the beautiful, good, and true. You find yourself living the bliss of dreams coming true. With flowing actions and attitude, bliss is yours now.

LINE 1: Flow back to wholeness.

I flow back to wholeness.

LINE 2: Let big goals go. Allow. Just as small springs fill big lakes, enjoy gentle flowing progress. You spontaneously realize your dreams now. This nonattachment frees you from the frustration of expectation and disappointment, and simultaneously allows for the hand of Spirit to direct events toward the greater good.

I let go of big goals into doing small parts and thus gently realize those big goals in detached joy.

LINE 3: Allow yourself the calming reassurance that it is right to rest. Know that nonaction is best now. You will reawaken to right moments for right action.

Now is the time for me to flow into valuable rest.

LINE 4: In extreme moments, formalities can be set aside. Authenticity matters most at such times. Inner truth will be quickly transferred from one to another. Begin with the most simple, clear, and obvious, and move forward step by step.

Knowing that extreme moments call for setting aside formalities, I act from authentic care and caring.

LINE 5: Now is a time to be content with simple steering around obstacles. It is too much to expect great accomplishments at the present. This is too far, too fast. Flowing slowly with what comes naturally frees you. Thus, great accomplishments come with ease and grace over time.

As I slowly flow with what comes naturally rather than push too far too fast, great accomplishments come with ease and grace.

LINE 6: Flowing joyfully with what is creates heavenly reality.

I flow joyfully with what is, bringing heavenly reality.

30. Passion, Fire, Connection

I fire my passion
with what fulfills me.

 Connecting, Fire
Connecting, Fire

Fire, passion, clings to its fuel. Connect to what feeds your passion. Stay steadily connected with what you care about most. Enrich your consciousness, attention, awareness, and experience. Your passion will radiate.

Success is nothing compared to fulfillment. What is the difference? Success, as used here, refers to reaching personal goals; fulfillment refers to contributing to the good of the whole. Success is good and okay, and empowers you to be able to give to others. But when you reach a level where you are focused on the good of the whole, rather than mere ego satisfaction, the knowing yourself as a center of goodness and love fills you with a glow that far surpasses personal goals. You realize a fulfillment day to day, moment to moment, that is far beyond previous levels of joy and meaning in your life.

With this knowledge of the passion to support the good of the whole, know that it serves the whole to integrate with self-care so you remain healthy and able to sustain serving the whole.

From this connected state, you transcend ego. You become one with nature and with others in ways that nurture you, everyone, and everything. Your existence unfolds naturally with flow and grace. Have you ever become joyously absorbed in an activity and come out feeling more whole and refreshed? This is pure passionate connection to life. Dive into your passion for goodness, your fire to give, to create, to evolve, and to make things better for everyone with a joy and energy that expresses a greater, higher you.

With benevolent, passionate connection, the following are now yours—wholeness, healing, health, creativity, contribution, prosperity, happiness, joy, love, and more.

LINE 1: Take time at the start to be clear, organized, and calm. Clarity at the beginning brings success in the end.

Starting well, I end well.

LINE 2: It is a time of greatness through centered balance; you achieve the highest expression, synchronizing sight, sound, and sentiment. To sustain this blessed state, it may help to visualize being centered in a cocoon of protective golden light radiating in balance to and from you.

I persevere in light combining the golden mean and Spiritual wholeness.

LINE 3: The time of sunset arrives. Be neither saddened nor self-indulging. Stay balanced and whole; you continue to realize the greatest good. All times can be lamented, overindulged, or, best of all, simply met with savoring calm wholeness. Have no judgments, no expectations, just experience.

I remain whole as I approach the end of a productive period.

LINE 4: Slow steady progress, not flaming out, realizes great goals. Stay steady and pure, connected to what's higher in each moment. No worry, no stress, progress with simple straightforward movement. Allow the inner light to lighten and enlighten each step. As you savor each moment, great good comes spontaneously. You do not need to know everything;

just what's right, right now. As you listen to your heart's guidance, you will know what's needed.

By listening to my heart, I persevere in slow, steady constructive focus savoring exquisite existence and unfolding results.

LINE 5: Cling to the vision of completed joys. Focused calm perseverance brings joy while creating dreams coming true. All adversity gives way to success, wholeness, happiness, and health.

Joy comes as I stay centered in visions of beautiful completed realities.

LINE 6: In self-discipline and self-development, be vigorous in extinguishing the truly negative replacing with the truly positive. Yet be not so strict with those things that do no harm to give you the freedom to be your unique self. Similarly accept uniqueness in others.

I am rigorous in ridding myself of genuine negativity and accepting of the rest that defines the unique me. I give others the same acceptance.

31. All Win

*I relate from and respond to
benevolent influence.*

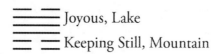 Joyous, Lake
Keeping Still, Mountain

Keeping your mind quiet and still, you arrive where the air is clearest at the lake of joy on top of the mountain. A clear mind is an open channel to divine guidance. The lake represents soothing wisdom. Stillness receives ultimate good. Joy is the result.

With openness and receptivity, you attain joy through following inner wisdom.

Calm joy outlasts giddiness. Just as being able to see through to depths of a pond needs a quiet surface, being able to see through to one's own inner depths calls for gentle joy not agitated excess. Keeping outer joy serene sustains the necessary stillness for deep lasting joy. All is well.

LINE 1: As a new influence shows itself, carefully, slowly, deliberately observe its effects. Only continue to commit time and resources to those things that nourish you and others, and release the rest.

I focus on what flows well and accept and let go of the rest.

LINE 2: Patiently wait until you definitely intuitively know what you want.

I calmly await knowing and then proceed.

LINE 3: Suspending the misperception of absolute necessity supports equanimity. Follow only influences you intuit will be good. To that end, wait and see how things develop. Rather than trying to exert undue influence, be natural, flow with events, and see what influences arise spontaneously. If the influence is good, proceed. If not, stop. Limits often apply. Freedom comes not only from the ability to go forward, but also from the ability and willingness to hold back.

I let go of the negative influence of absolute necessity, holding back until I gain a clear vision of what flows well and then follow that path. I enjoy the added freedom of holding back from what does not flow well.

LINE 4: Truth and goodness from the heart spread far and wide without conscious effort. Discern spontaneous innocent influence from attempts to control. The latter limits; the former sets one free.

I discern and follow authentic goodness.

LINE 5: Choose the optimal course guided by wisdom within. Act with independence, purity and goodwill. Be receptive to all three.

I choose the optimal course: independence, purity, and goodwill.

LINE 6: Mere talk has little value. Influence and be influenced by good deeds.

In both influencing and being influenced, I forego talk in favor of actions.

32. Enduring Progress

*Unhurried calm savoring
creates joyful steady progress.*

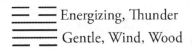 Energizing, Thunder
Gentle, Wind, Wood

Big goals and visions inspire you like a massive storm as implied by wind and thunder. Remain calm in the storm. Stay gentle. The best results flow from a calm centered mind. Cultivate equanimity. Stay serene while you create. Maintain peaceful poise, posture, pace, and perspective. Drink in life unfolding. Embrace a sense of savoring each moment, each step, that eventually leads to goal after goal blossoming in its own time in smooth flow and excellence. Coast uphill.[8]

Embrace the growth cycles of life, your life, your visions. Let go of expectations into presence. Be the calm center you want to be. Watch your dreams unfold.

An optimal state of mind to meet all challenges is: no judgments, no expectations, no attachments, only experience.[9]

Enjoy the beauty of each step, each phase from bud to blossom to full flowering. See the sparkle of life in each era. Don't hurry to the end and miss the good on the way, the joy of the journey, the essence of life.

Give yourself ease and calm. Give yourself time and energy to interact with each person, place, and thing of beauty, life, and love. Relate in ways that nourish your and others' souls. Follow natural unfolding.

Savor your life. This is it, every day, every hour, every moment. Loving others and serving them, while maintaining healthy boundaries, is among life's greatest gifts. This is what you came for. Enjoy it.

Practice total presence and single-pointed focused awareness in each moment to increase safety and effectiveness.

LINE 1: Be calm and steady. Stay peaceful and composed. Do not attempt to go too far too fast. Cultivate slow perseverance in deep equanimity and all is well.

I restrain rushing in favor of slow savoring.

LINE 2: Gentle progress from deep tranquility creates new results. Don't overdo. Persevere inner and outer progress in quiet calm.

I cultivate deep calm continual progress.

LINE 3: Create duration of character. Meet external ups and downs with equanimity. Know spiritual peace in your heart; here is all power to forbear and do well in all things. Such equanimity underlies enduring confidence. Underlying such confidence is regular connection within, as you are doing now in direct dialogue with Spirit. To dialogue directly with Spirit, be in a meditative state in a safe quiet space; ask within and listen for the answers that come from pure Source in receptive suspension of disbelief.

I cultivate enduring character in deep spiritual equanimity.

LINE 4: You cannot find what you seek where it is not. Externals, artificial spirituality, and only immediate pleasure do not yield wholeness, inner peace, and fulfillment. These good things come from deep within. From the well of goodness within, bring the good outward nurturing those about you and yourself. Empty eyes find false fulfillment in intoxicants whether chemical or behavioral. Full eyes radiate hearts immersed in pure goodness, touched within expressing outward.

It is possible to transform from empty to full. First, choose to do so. Then, quietly look and listen within for the best and highest in you. Because you are human, it is there. Search your soul in quiet inner focus for that which inspires and moves you. Act upon the wisdom you gain. This manifesting good carries you all the way home to the heart of joy, meaning, and love of life.

I am fulfilled as I find and express good from within outward.

LINE 5: To preserve mind over emotion, let constructive thoughts produce positive feelings and results. Allow others their ways and keep evolving your own. With new information and circumstances, shift how you approach things including the tasks you take on or delegate, remaining true to what's good.

My wholeness comes from moving forward.[10]

LINE 6: A pool of clear still water allows you to see the bottom. Likewise a calm, clear mind allows you to see through to your core. The essence of the infinite within can be seen, felt and heard, as you stay calm and whole. Avoid restless pushing and striving. In its place, cultivate calm inner connection. Then all things ultimately bless you.

I connect to infinite joy through calm clarity that comes from inner stillness.

33. Retreat and Renew

I withdraw to higher ground
seeding my soul in rest and retreat.

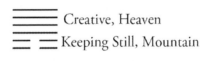 Creative, Heaven
Keeping Still, Mountain

As you keep still within, allow the healing magnetism of inner light to purify you. Be still and allow the inner light to heal you. Deep quiet puts you in touch with heaven within. Open to benevolent being.

Now is a time to retreat; not act, not try. The door to what's better for you now opens with gentle withdrawal. There is perfection in this ease. It is easy to see, decide, and do. There is no confusion. This is the best course.

Take heart. This withdrawal is to higher ground. Now is a good time to incubate. You shall return refreshed and energized. Retreat is a way station, not a permanent destination. Resting now generates a firmer foundation for the future. You regain strength for creativity and joy. Linger here in repose as internal and external conditions rearrange without taxing you.

Optimally optimize the optimum. Synchronize and harmonize with what is in each moment. Embrace inner peace in relation to each circumstance as it arises.

Feel gentle goodness strongly entering you. In quiet retreat, gain peace of mind. Surround the beautiful being that you are and are becoming with healing self-acceptance and profound self-love.

Self-love is the opposite of selfishness, because you nourish yourself independent of others and regenerate so you ultimately have more to give.

Presently lay burdens down. Rest, retreat, heal, and welcome wholeness. Retreat and be free. Rest and build abilities to respond later. You will be in a stronger place to connect deeply with the good in life. You gain freedom from negative reactions to life's challenges. Still better, you will be able to meet challenges in positive perspective and gain even greater benefit than had the challenge never occurred. Look for the gifts in the challenges.

Allow a warm, gentle benevolence to envelop you, particularly in the area of your solar plexus, your emotional center. Let this wholeness rise to your heart. Picture, feel, and manifest, goodness. Be in and of it. From this fertile center, embrace oneness with life. Melt away hardness, fear and all whisper of failure. You are seeding your soul to sing. You will blossom in time to come.

LINE 1: Gently move your attention from letting go without to embracing stillness within. Connecting with negative forces brings decline. Replace external involvement with total release into inner light. All will work out better than you dared hope as you cease participating. This extinguishes any expectations of response from you.

In letting go of outward focus, I allow my attention to float gently inward, "Be still and know I am God."

LINE 2: Without, complete disengagement. Within, complete connection. Connection to higher consciousness. Quiet confidence that all is well makes it so.

Total outer release and inner connection bring peace now.

LINE 3: Avoid entanglement in commitments beyond your scope.
It is problematic when you find yourself wanting to be free of such
overcommitment. How to do this is to commit only to those things you
truly want in your deepest heart. Adopt the humility to know your limits
and you remain free, happy, and prosperous.

*I remain free and happy by knowing and acting in accord with my
limited capacity and deepest hopes.*

LINE 4: Nonresistance means there is nothing for inferior forces to push
against. In nonresistance, you remain free. Inferior consciousness, within
or without, will appropriately be left with the responsibility to realize and
evolve itself.

*In goodwill, I retreat from all that is inferior within and without. With
lack of energy, the inferior ceases, thus ushering in greater goodness.*

LINE 5: Realize that a series of attempts will be launched to draw you back
into undesirable states of being. Be kind, yet consistent in steady retreat.
Clean, clear separation frees you to realize great heights waiting on the
wings as you assure your freedom by becoming one with the light within.
Knowing it's not personal helps bring healing wholeness to all concerned.

*I accept that it is natural for some to test my resolve to avoid being hooked
into negativity. As I hold such tests as opportunities to demonstrate my resolve,
the tests cease and I evolve along with circumstances.*

LINE 6: By establishing physical and psychological distance, you have
worked hard and well to win much deserved freedom. Remain free with
goodwill and finesse. Staying happy helps. Clear vision ahead keeps
you on the path. Respect and allow others to reap their own karma and
the invaluable soul shaping that comes with it. To return to carrying
the problems of others serves neither of you. To move on joyfully and
graciously serves everyone, especially you.

*I preserve my hard won and profoundly valuable freedom with
empowering and appropriate social distance.*

34. Wise Restraint Retains Great Power

Limiting myself to what's higher,
I preserve power for good.

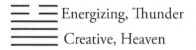 Energizing, Thunder
Creative, Heaven

Heavenly creativity is energized by thunder. Thunder indicates one has great influence. This profound combination can be seductive leading to rash actions from desire to experience power. The greater your power, the greater your ability to create good or ill.

With the great power you have now, you create heaven within and without aligning with the beautiful, good, and true. Align your thoughts, actions, and consequent feelings, especially when you experience challenge.

With much power comes the responsibility to use it wisely, or pay dearly in creating results you would not want. Choose wisely, with compassion and care. Right action results from clarity. Attend to information from crucial sources—your senses, gut instinct, clear thinking, wise counsel, and, most of all, higher guidance.

Great power calls for caution. When you are quiet enough to hear the small voice within, the heart counsels tenderness with meaning and passion. Do what is best for all, including you. But if your focus is on yourself alone, it is obvious to all. Others withdraw. You lose your power.

Imagine driving a giant truck on a highway. You would want to proceed at a safe rate, slow enough to match your driving skills and road conditions, and fast enough to flow with traffic. Given such power, you could literally move mountains. This is the situation you are in now. Be sure any mountains you choose to move are worth the effort before you move them. If the answer is yes, move those mountains carefully. In the process, stay focused on balance.

Great power and influence are now yours. You may use them to create heaven on earth for others and yourself in gracious movement toward the beautiful, good, and true. Blessed be your contemplations, choices, and actions. Consciously harmonize them as they determine what you create, who you are, and who you become.

Line 1: Attempted advance by force or cunning creates the opposite of what you want. At the first sign of nonacceptance, disengagement is your best option. Be guided by inner wisdom, not by ego or externals. Return to higher intentions, to your higher self.

I disengage wisely at the first sign of nonacceptance. Pushing onward creates greater resistance.

Line 2: The way begins to open. Proceed with calm equanimity, not with overenthusiastic self-confidence which may lead to mistakes. Gentle step-by-step perseverance works best.

As the way opens, I persevere in gentle humility.

Line 3: Restrain yourself in relationships from outer destructive confrontations. Hold back until you are certain your actions are right, good, and will result in a positive outcome for all. To succeed outwardly, develop inwardly. Cease being little. Withdraw and work on yourself until gracious behavior becomes an authentic expression of your inner state.

Rather than repressing reactivity, truly transform through compassion and wisdom.

I hold back until I have clear, calm inner knowing expressing itself in outer quiet confidence.

LINE 4: You will succeed by gently removing obstacles one at a time. Less effort and more wisdom serves you well. You create more with less. You undo doubt and proceed with ease. Excellence is yours.

I proceed using more wisdom and less energy.

LINE 5: Substitute higher, softer thoughts, feelings, and actions for lower, harder ones. When you soften obstacles are removed. The way opens before you.

The softer I express, the more I accomplish.

LINE 6: Gently progress. If you attempt to go too far too fast, things stop flowing. Hardness worsens problems. Return to serenity. Listen to inner guidance, sensing each best next step, doing it and then the next and so on, in a calm, easy, joyful flow. Things will go well as if by magic. You enjoy getting there. And the quality of what you create is higher.

I proceed with a calm, easy, joyful flow enjoying the journey more than the goals.

35. You Rise Like the Sun

I flow with pure heart
and clear vision.

 Connecting, Fire
Receptive, Earth

The image of the sun rising high over the earth indicates you will rise naturally with flow and grace. Because you have purity of purpose and right action, all goes well.

Create great value in this opportune time. Prioritize and do the highest first. Give top priority to what creates and contributes the most consuming the least. Slow, conscious, and steady creates best with the least effort and fewest mistakes.

There is infinite joy in simple work. Compatible people create in mutual joy. Be so. Create such times. Enjoy creating this mutual joy.

LINE 1: Resist not resistors. Simply, gently proceed in quiet self-confidence in right, good actions from your higher self. As you listen within to higher guidance, you constantly improve doing better things, at better times, in better ways.

Rather than resist, I persist in higher nature.

LINE 2: The higher self wants to express through you now. Sense and follow the inner light for the greatest joy, creativity, and contribution. Fulfill your dreams and purpose, your reason for being. Coordinate with others in humility for greatest progress.

I express inner light now.

LINE 3: Worry not where your skills, stamina, or resources seem to fall short of the task at hand. Enroll others of good graces to participate, mentor, and assist you. All benefit.

I relax into receiving help when I could use it and others want to give it.

LINE 4: When things go well, avoid arrogance. Modesty sustains success. In times of progress, those acting from lower intentions succeed at first, yet eventually decline. Purity alone sustains progress.

I preserve progress through purity and humility.

LINE 5: Allow momentary ups and downs without worry or excessive effort. Flow with faith and confidence. Let go of past regrets. Keep only the wisdom gained.

I learn from past mistakes, and otherwise let go of self-punishment and worry, and allow things to flow forward.

LINE 6: Eliminate fear, doubt, and anger. Be hard on your own negativity and easy on others. Life will correct their errors. When you emphasize faith, confidence, and acceptance, you prevent the need for life to correct you.

I let go of fear, doubt, and anger. I correct my own mistakes and let life correct others.

36. Brighten Within

I embrace the light within.

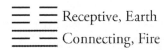 Receptive, Earth
Connecting, Fire

The connecting fire within the receptive earth means brightening your inner light despite outer challenges. When it's dark outside, brighten within in solitude. Outer circumstances may not be exactly as you prefer them. When it is difficult to change outer circumstances, quickly and quietly brighten within allowing outer challenges to cycle through without pulling your spirit down, without getting caught in a downward spiral.

The quiet safe haven of your inner light is available now. The key to opening inner doors is staying connected to the Divine. Keep things small. Slow and simple is preferred now. From this connection, evolve the meaning you read into circumstances through calm contemplation.

Circumstances sometimes just are. The meaning you assign to them has great power. When you create meaning in concert with divine will, you optimize existence. To be connected to the Divine, become aware of the *I Am* that you are, a living part of the whole. Bring present focus out of fear of future, and out of resentment or shame of the past. Ask *who is having these feelings,* then experience the answer.

Contemplate the meaning of these words. Experience yourself as pure presence. Since you are life itself, this inner connection puts you in touch with all life, with the Divine. Direct your attention to the present, to your breath, to your witness consciousness, to your attention itself.

By aligning with the divine, you align with ultimate power and goodness; you will ultimately succeed and be fulfilled. You are welcome at every moment to this experience. A similar path to connection is to *be still and know that I am God,* a part of the ever evolving universe.

From this connected, aligned place choosing to see challenge as opportunity moves you in that direction by your active choice. You put yourself in an empowered, proactive position. You are being a creator in your own life. As you align with the Divine, you can only succeed. The constructive meanings you make of circumstances become real.

As you empower yourself, making positive, spiritually connected meaning of challenges, you are more able to constructively affect outer conditions. You learn and become more in the process. You increase your wisdom and strengthen your skill. You handle similar situations better. People respect and appreciate you more and treat you better.

You even come to enjoy challenge as it brings increasing effectiveness and ability. Circumstances that previously brought frustration, fear, sadness, or anger bring success, gladness, and joy. You see yourself in a new light because you have truly transcended. Good comes that would not, had the challenges been absent.

When you are emotionally triggered, a way to get through the challenge is to stay as calm as you can. Keep bringing yourself back from the story you are telling yourself. This story is what is triggering you. Simply return to what you are sensing in the present moment.

As you brighten inside, you gain, grow, and increase enjoyment of your own company, your own life, and the effect you have on others.

LINE 1: To break through to wholeness, to inner connection to life, to inner peace and ultimately joy, clarify what's not negotiable. Create ways to harmoniously include this in your decisions, speech, and actions.

I discern and persevere in the pure and good.

LINE 2: Although the problem is difficult for you, it is crucial for others. If in your solving your difficulties, you care for the concerns of others, you succeed, are blessed and can proceed with your life whole and supported by divine will.

I realize others may have it harder than I do. I take their concerns into consideration as I resolve my challenges.

LINE 3: Fortunately you see through to the root of the problem. Because it has been longstanding, it takes a bit of time and effort to undo. Persevere and all will clear with trust in inner guidance and confidence in yourself.

Understanding deeply, I take the necessary time and care required for resolution. Taking the time brings me independence and self-confidence.

LINE 4: Disengage from others who exhibit intentions that would harm. Do so with goodwill and caring. But do so with alacrity and finesse that frees you quickly, cleanly, and totally. They then have greater opportunity to transcend negativity.

I allow myself, the situation, and others to transform by quickly and carefully removing myself from harm's way

LINE 5: Finding yourself in a limited situation, keep a happy heart. Find the meaning and message in circumstances for you in this time. Integrate the wisdom in how you are, what you do, and what you do not do. Compromise not with those of ill intentions when they are in an overpowering position. Be outwardly cordial, yet stay free within to support the good of the whole and work your way increasingly free without.

I remain free and self-determined to pursue good by being cordial externally while firm within.

LINE 6: Disengage from inner and outer negativity. When left alone, negativity undoes itself. Embrace positive energy and attitude. You will create profound rapid shifts for the better.

I align with the Divine and let the rest resolve itself, which it ultimately will.

37. LOVED ONES

I relate from love, not fear.

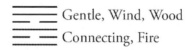 Gentle, Wind, Wood
Connecting, Fire

F ire clings to its fuel. Gentle wind feeds the fire further, giving it oxygen, giving it life. You may connect directly to this Source by calling forth and generating the experience of love to and from everyone and everything. Gently remain devoted to your Source, to those closest to you, to your family, to your clan. Keep the fire of caring relationships burning within the family that keeps it alive.

A healthy family is maintained with constant words of encouragement and wisdom. Wise words that also encourage are Spirit-realized. To inspire means to bring in Spirit. Let the words you think, your thoughts, be kind, wise and gentle. Then the words you speak will follow.

When contemplating family, include immediate family all the way to the entire human family and to the earth and all living beings.

Wisdom balances love, kindness, affection, and concern about the well being of others and the family as a whole. Wisdom balances freedom, fairness, and firmness. Great families have great leaders. Leadership is freely passed to those in the best position to guide in given moments.

In functional families, each member easily shifts to appropriate roles as circumstances change. Be willing to harmonize with what's needed now. Healthy family leadership comes from inspiration, example, and respect. Each person is empowered.

A harmonious world is built from harmonious families. Harmonious families come from constant improvement of self and circumstances, from delineation of expectations, roles, duties, obligations and freedoms mixed with healthy portions of fun, affection, work, play, and rest.

As you are called upon to lead, stay tuned to inner wisdom. A simple way is to ask your heart what is good now. Listen and respond to what Spirit brings to mind. Be sure that you are listening to Spirit and not ego. Asking what's best for all helps discern the two.

LINE 1: Allow love in the beginning, middle, and end. With love, the firmness necessary for harmonious self-discipline works. Discipline of self and lower urges, discipline of children, when surrounded by a field of love creates the firmness necessary for harmony within the family and beyond. When children know love, they want to contribute to what's best for all in the family. To the extent love is withheld, desire to contribute is blocked. Sometimes love of self or others is holding back rather than giving in, but it always celebrates the existence of the other. This being celebrated, this validation generates in everyone the inner desire for self-discipline.

As I express loving validation, I cultivate harmonious relationships and inspire others to choose healthy self-discipline.

LINE 2: Each of us following our own inner heartbeat and allowing others to do the same creates the best family and world.

As I encourage freedom, I support excellence.

LINE 3: Be neither too soft nor too hard. Within broad yet definite limits, allow others freedom to find their own way. Then all will be well. For smaller frustrations, temporary upset is to be expected in life; just don't hold on to it. Let go and move on to more harmonious times as soon as possible. For deeper issues requiring more attention, take the responsibility to handle them in calm, caring competence. Allow varying views to be heard, validated, and integrated into an all-win wholeness. Great progress, growth, learning, and success come of this.

I listen, validate, and integrate others' concerns with careful and caring wisdom.

LINE 4: Nurture each other while preserving resources and all will be well. When expending resources, do so in ways that they are replaced. Recycle what would otherwise be waste into renewed resources. Then you will not want.

I consciously nurture nature as I nurture others and myself.

LINE 5: Love, not fear, is the best basis of leadership in the family and everywhere else.

I lead from and with love within and outside family.

LINE 6: To influence others, develop yourself. They will know the truth of your goodness and follow your lead from knowing it's the best thing to do. Success comes to families and all groups from following leaders of goodwill, wisdom, integrity, and love.

I lead with goodwill, wisdom, integrity, and love.

38. Broaden Perspectives

I create great gains
by broadening my perspective.

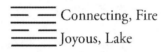 Connecting, Fire
Joyous, Lake

The water of the lake and the clinging fire are opposites. Opposites can repel, or they can broaden; you have the power to choose which. You increase your joy when you choose broadening. Choosing to expand by valuing and harmonizing differences, you increase your wisdom, effectiveness, peace of mind, and relationships.

You control your experience of the facts by the meaning you assign them. Taking a broader view, embracing differences of opinion as enlightening, you counter inner resistance and resentment; two forces which defeat goals. Resistance creates counter resistance and pushes things in the opposite direction you are seeking. Resentment spoils joy and makes you ineffective.

When you allow deep truth from various sources to seep into your soul, you expand the spiritual benefit you receive and give. Gentle, calm, mutual consideration in a spirit of goodwill, mutual benefit, and open mindedness creates better conditions and solutions for all than had the opposition never occurred. Picture, if you will, how healthy competitive sports inspire and increase joy, health, and companionship.

Ultimately success and failure is what we each define them to be. An optimally empowering perspective is to embrace and welcome learning and growing. Accepting what exists opens opportunities. Embracing reality and defining what is as what's supposed to be, you empower yourself. Positive influence and constant improvement arise with acceptance. You give yourself the breadth to handle a wide range of events and do the best each moment.

Accepting what is as okay, you experience the greatest possible joy in the circumstances, adding to your health and power to create good. Creating powerful good with joy makes a great life of harmony, contribution, and fulfillment.

Even temporary things you do not like, and everything is ultimately temporary, give you valuable information about what is desirable. The most negative experiences can be positive defining moments. By embracing apparently negative circumstances as valuable information, you create contrasting clarity to see what you do like. And you generate energy to bring those things about. You use contrary experience to evolve.

Being open to whatever comes, expands opportunity. Overcoming inner resistance is one of the most empowering things you can do. Overcoming inner resistance undoes the debilitating, depressing, and character dissolving effects of cynicism.

To overcome inner opposition, look to your long-term visions. There is an optimal way to bring these visions into reality. Plan small steps, prioritize the steps, and keep moving ahead one step at a time. Incubating may be one of the steps in creating dreams coming true; this may call for allowing circumstances and clarity time to mature before taking the next step.

Have patience. Do other things in the meantime. Allowing things to develop with ease, clarifies and facilitates any doing needed.

To influence another, listen well first. Be as an empty vessel, open and receptive. Be respectful. Clearly understand the other's ideas and interests. Align with them by cocreating visions, goals, and means that also nurture you and all concerned in mutual goodwill. You will be rewarded in fact and feelings. You will be a low maintenance person. As a low maintenance person, you leverage your life circumstances into greater joy, happiness, and success. In short you will be attractive, effective, and happy.

Where differences remain, set healthy limits in a kind and effective manner, and create sufficient space for the differences to peacefully coexist.

By cocreating shared goals and sufficient space to accommodate what's outside the goals, you experience things going well with less stress. By combining caring commitment with detachment, you optimize the way. What will actually be happening is greater still. You will sometimes get your way plain and simple, sometimes integrate your way with others' for greater solutions and harmony than otherwise would have happened, and sometimes, you will defer to circumstances or others' greater wisdom, greater influence, or both. Sometimes there will be circumstances beyond your control, and you will learn and grow in the process with minimum cost and maximum benefit. In all cases, you gain more with less effort. Gaining more with less effort is a core process in creating prosperity, joy, and harmony while having a meaningful life.

LINE 1: Allow differences. People and things you want to unite will return naturally. With people and things you do not want to connect, neither resist nor indulge, and they will go away naturally. Use no forcing.

I don't push. I allow. All goes well.

LINE 2: With an open heart and mind, spontaneous resolutions evolve.

In openness, I create peace of mind.

LINE 3: Although things seem to not be working, they are. Everything happens for good reason. Synchronize with what is and work your way step-by-step to a place where all concerned benefit. You gain too. Listen to your heart's messages. Your heart will guide you well to the one best answer that nurtures you and all others.

By accepting what is, knowing everything happens for good reason, and practicing all win, I reap many rewards, the greatest being inner peace.

LINE 4: Sometimes one can be alone and isolated from others. But if you find one other person who shares your understanding, it is all resolved. Seek out and find a compatible companion when you are feeling disconnected. The companion may be another person or higher nature, through meditation or by consulting written wisdom that moves you like the *I Ching*.

I find mutuality in companionship with another person, nature, inspiring writing, or meditation.

LINE 5: When initial connections go poorly, give things time and space, and those that are harmonious will eventually come forward.

I allow time and space for mutuality to manifest.

LINE 6: Inner turmoil can lead to misreading the positive intentions of others. See others good intentions by first resolving your own inner conflicts.

I do not misread positive intentions of others as a result of my own issues; I resolve these first.

39. The Way Around

*I flow around challenges
with wisdom, kindness, and joy.*

 Open Space, Water
Keeping Still, Mountain

As a stream flowing from a deep spring within an ancient mountain is secure in its source, connect within your own depths to find the way. Let resolution after resolution flow like crystal clear water from within to without.

How does one connect with inner stillness? Whenever you encounter challenge, ask *who is experiencing this as challenge?* Experience the experiencer; witness the witness. Witness with your heart with love. This witness is your deep sacred self, your consciousness. This consciousness is unified with all consciousness, the home of wisdom, equanimity, wholeness, and healing.

If you are feeling psychological frustration or physical pain, first identify with the witness, then ask if the witness is feeling the frustration or pain. From this open, nonreactive presence, you empower yourself as you contemplate the specifics of your opportunity.

Let deep healing be attracted by your challenges. Thus, transform problems into life-giving magnetic purpose, meaning, health and happiness.

You, as a human being, are endowed with the power to manage the meaning you make of events. If you set your meaning making process to instantly respond creatively when unexpected challenges arise, you make the best of whatever happens. You respond rather than react. You own your personal power to affect events in the most constructive way possible.

A general mind-set for all challenges is to hold the perspective that whatever arises, the challenge can and will be a learning-empowering experience. This point of view makes it precisely so through self-fulfilling prophecy. The calmness of acceptance and even embracing unexpected events puts you in a frame of mind to meet them with optimal wisdom, goodwill, and presence. In your calm competence, you become a beacon of inspiration, not only to others, but also to your former self.

This new mind-set of being prepared to embrace the unexpected shifts you from fear to love. Rather than putting yourself in a position where all sorts of undesirable things happen to you, the position of victim, you create yourself as a creator. You proactively generate your experiences to be colorful, adventurous, fascinating, and expanding. Who you are essentially changes. You become attractive to yourself, and hence to others. Life holds attraction for you rather than dread. All kinds of new and delicious experiences are yours.

Take your time. Gather resources. Include as essential rest and repose. Gather wisdom from the wisest counselors. Wisdom brings the greatest fulfillment. Proceed accordingly with a light step and in good spirits. Though your challenges may have increased ten-fold, with the joyful flow of resolving, your wisdom, power, and joy are multiplied a thousand-fold.

To take light yet effective steps, realize that *what you are* is simply the *awareness that is here* now.[11]

Congratulations, you are growing in health, happiness, and wealth as you flow around and through challenges with wisdom with joy.

LINE 1: Upon first encountering an obstruction, the best first thing to do is to study the obstruction from the perspective of acceptance. Seeking the opportunity, the gift in the challenge, there is great value to be gained. Thus shifting to a positive perspective about what you might otherwise hold negatively creates generative energy for creating a better existence had the obstruction not occurred in the first place. In this contemplation, retreat, sense the best pace, means, and timing to respond well, not reactively, and proceed accordingly. You continuously improve the situation yourself gaining knowledge, skill, wisdom, and joy.

I embrace apparent obstructions when they first arise knowing this will transform to great benefit.

LINE 2: The best usual approach to an obstruction is to allow it to be and take time to study the best way around it. There are times though, when immediate action is called for. Even though we are not to blame, to remain blame free, we need to take wise effective action in a timely manner. Discerning when such is the case and when not and proceeding accordingly is a serious matter. Consulting inner wisdom in authentic openness to divine guidance with confidence proves to be a blessing in handling such challenges well. Furthermore, ask for, receive, and pass on the energy of divine guidance. As you pass the healing energy of the divine to heal the obstruction, you too are healed. If you get this line and sense you are faced with such a challenge, you may ask the oracle once again how to proceed.

When immediate response is necessary, I respond in a timely manner, and with the best guidance available.

LINE 3: Restrain yourself. Accept. Cultivate equanimity. When equanimity is deeply achieved, it is the time to address the problems and not before. You will transform and you will handle the problem well.

When confronted with challenge, I first cultivate equanimity, and then proceed in the best possible frame of mind.

LINE 4: Stillness, inner focus, faith and patience attract the right helpers and the best solutions at the right time and no sooner.

From inner stillness, I sense and wait for the best time to act.

LINE 5: Hang in there, but do it in the right way with calm, wisdom, gratitude, and graciousness. You may be on the path to your greatest contribution and calling. People may be in deep need of this service. You will succeed greatly only if you proceed in kind, caring, skill and equanimity. In the meantime, take care of your personal emotional needs privately.

I persevere in calm wholeness with each new happening and thereby harvest great value from all experience.

LINE 6: You have conquered greater obstacles. You have enjoyed helping others in the process. You have sought and received excellent counsel. You were rewarded in all such cases. Continue serving and continue to receive great reward.

Having received great rewards from serving, as I continue to give, I continue to receive.

40. FREEDOM

As I accept and forgive myself and others, I am free.

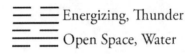Energizing, Thunder
Open Space, Water

Rain and thunder make thunderstorms. Thunderstorms wash the air clean. New attitudes resolve. Gently persevere until all is done and you are whole again.

Freedom comes from clearing your consciousness. Forgiving, accepting, embracing learning and your higher nature all leave you free. Don't cry over spilt milk, but do clean it up and learn from it.

Forgiving mistakes of others frees you from poisoning yourself with your own bitterness. Forgiving frees you from misconduct yourself. It puts an end to downward cycles of depression and violence. Forgiving begins upward spirals of peace within and without, of joy and wholeness.

Forgiving yourself for false beliefs that you are not okay frees you from the core of suffering.[12]

Accepting what is and what has been prevents the return of maliciousness from and toward you. Acceptance opens you to gaining value from the storms you weather. It would be sad to go through them and yet gain nothing. Accepting creates calm, whole equanimity.

Embracing learning from the trials you endure gives you meaning and wisdom. You acquire new skills. You respond more competently in future similar situations, resolving potential issues before they become unmanageable.

Disengaging from negative influences within and without in calm wholeness frees you.

Forgiving, accepting, learning, and lovingly disengaging from negative attitudes and relationships, newness emerges lighting, lightening, and enlightening you. You are brighter and more joyous. Things weigh less on you. And you become smarter. Storms clear. You awaken within. Inner connections to your higher self are strengthened and you are deeply nourished.

LINE 1: The issue is resolved. Inner conflict is transcended. Remain peaceful, in loving goodwill, and all remains well. As you embrace this peace, you open more and more to healing energy dwelling in and around you.

All is well; I embrace all.

LINE 2: Deliverance from trouble comes with relinquishing lower motivations in favor of higher. Gently withdraw from what you know is self-defeating. Free yourself from depending on others, things, or circumstances being different for you to be whole and happy. Simply focus on self-nourishing. You free yourself and life flows as you follow the pure, good, and simple.

As I follow the pure, good, and simple, I am released, free.

LINE 3: Once having the humility and wisdom to align with what's beautiful, good, and true and doing your part, things improve. You lose these gains if you become arrogant putting yourself above others. All this impedes your contribution. Remain humble; continue your contribution and your success is certain.

Humility continues successes.

Line 4: Freeing yourself from the lower makes room for the higher. At times one may slide into viewpoints and relationships that inhibit higher existence. Releasing lower attitudes and connections opens the way for higher ones.

I release what's lower into what's higher.

Line 5: To be truly rid of negative influences, you must completely disconnect from them. Only then do these issues cease.

I am truly free as I disconnect from all negative—within and without.

Line 6: Complete innocence and purity with no hidden agenda set you totally free. Letting go of judging others resolves the situation. At the same time being aware of hidden agendas, wrong actions, or negative judgments, and wisely stepping aside from them in humble innocence frees you and leaves the other to be corrected by life. This is certain.

I am free as I am innocent and let go of judging others.

41. Slowing Down

I slow down, savor, and save.

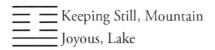
Keeping Still, Mountain
Joyous, Lake

Moderation supports equanimity and joy. Slowing without, increases joy within. There are times when life can be so intense that it helps to slow down. Keeping still at such times can be challenging. Be like a gentle old mountain. Be restful in the certainty of success. Know you are ultimately life itself. Know you will eventually return home to the bliss of all life. All will be all right for you forever. Know that you will ultimately achieve a state of being that fulfills your every desire.

To successfully navigate life, use brakes as well as the accelerator. For now, slow down and enjoy the journey as an individual soul adding to life. As an individual awareness, you are contributing to all consciousness. Realize that the richness of your experience here and now nurtures everything, including you, forever. Be in no hurry to be done here and now. Instead, be calm, conscious, and present. Gather gifts of serene love and joy.

This is a time to do less. Enjoy nature. Ponder wisdom, recline, relax, relate, and love. Your life is unfolding moment by moment. Don't miss it.

Drink it in. Savor the precious gifts, wisdom, beauty, joy, and above all, love.

LINE 1: Do your part. Support others to do theirs, but don't take the gift from them of doing their part. Both you and others are here to evolve and contribute. Manifest your highest being and support others doing the same. Hold back when others manifest lower nature. Ultimately, it helps to give you both space to live well. Live in your higher nature. Be an example and nurture the same in others.

I do my part and give others space to do their part.

LINE 2: Set valuable limits to avoid mistakes and excess tiredness. Be an example of self-nurturing to others. Avoid de-motivating others by doing their self-improvement work. Set healthy boundaries. In a Spirit of providing great value, let others pay you a fair price for your service, and thus allow yourself to keep serving. Ask your heart what is best in each moment. Tune into inner guidance for the best balance of what is most mutually nourishing for all. By doing these things you will prosper spiritually, materially, and in your relationships. If you err at all, err a bit on the side of giving and you will receive more and be more affluent in the flow of life, love, and all forms of prosperity.

I balance giving and receiving.

LINE 3: Where ego exits, Spirit enters. Slow down, soften inside. Reassuring energy and nurturing warmth bless you. Allow others to limit connection with you as you reach your own or their limits. Preserve precious pearls within. Get and stay right with your higher self, the light within. When praising, focus on others; when growing, focus on self.

In living healthy limits, I blossom.

LINE 4: Growing is great when you focus on your own development. As you decrease faults, replacing them with virtues, others approach and enhance you. You prevent problems when you focus on self-improvement rather than trying to change others.

In soaring self-improvement, I fly over the mud of trying to change others.

LINE 5: All goes well when you are innocent and pure. Intend and act for good only. Then there are no limits. Spirit can and will open unexpected opportunities that nourish you beyond expectations.

As I *think, act, and exist in pure goodness, all goes well.*

LINE 6: If, as you increase, you increase others, you benefit still further.

The more I share good fortune, the more my good fortune grows.

42. Profound Advance

Good times increase
as I nurture and give.

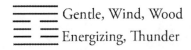 Gentle, Wind, Wood
Energizing, Thunder

A fundamental idea presented in the *I Ching* is the leader who serves. In this hexagram, the strong line beginning the upper trigram drops down to the beginning of the lower. Everyone advances when one in a higher position serves those below.

Two profound energies—thunder and wind—reinforce each other. The one above who serves those below receives joyful loyalty. Everyone benefits.

There is a temptation to decrease effort when progress is easy. Since times of easy progress come and go, do the opposite. When the way opens, continue moving forward with enthusiasm.

Benevolent times support good relations. Focusing on present successes dissolves past issues. It is easier to be forgiving when things are going well. If you do this, when challenging times return, you are better prepared. While, things are going well, use the positive energy of present successes to transcend previous difficulties.

Giving increases your own good fortune. Giving to others in opportune times invests present prosperity for times of lesser fortune. If you had no limits, would you not want to give generously? To increase limitlessness, give yourself the gift of giving.

When in a position to serve well, do so. Everyone benefits, including you. To sacrifice lower motivations to higher ones is the essence of self-improvement.

You are the primary creative force in your own life. What you create, you receive. One of life's greatest joys is serving and evolving in times of opportunity. Now is such a time. Serving the good, serving others, opens your heart, mind, and will. You and all about you prosper with great blessings.

LINE 1: Great good fortune is now yours. When you share your good fortune with others, it will remain and grow.

By sharing my good fortune, I advance while the way is open.

LINE 2: As you pursue true goodness, nothing holds you back.

As I seek true goodness, all things progress.

LINE 3: Make good out of what at first seemed otherwise. What may seem unfortunate turns out to be its opposite. You have the power to define challenges positively. Accepting what is, you align with events. You grow by harmonizing your will with reality. At times the good comes spontaneously. At other times, you can use the contrast of what's undesirable to clarify what's desirable. Then pursue the good energized by the contrast. With this mind-set, the more undesirable circumstances are, the greater the energy generated to create their opposite.

I exercise and energize my power of choice for good.

LINE 4: Bring good to others. You will be trusted and supported by those above, below, and in equal positions. Everyone increases.

I bring good to everyone and everyone benefits, including myself.

LINE 5: A truly kind person acts not for outer gain but from inner desire and choice to be kind. Cultivating a kind essence brings you to the center of your soul. Connection to the center of your soul is your link to Spirit. You live in blessed grace. You are known by the joyful calm you radiate. Benefit flows freely from you blessing all.

My choice to contribute and be kind adds to the evolution of all, more my own than any other.

LINE 6: You are in a position of power and prosperity because others helped you. If you selfishly attempt to keep all you have gained only for you and yours, you lose it and more. Those you support mirror your actions. You are blessed by the higher motivations of others. All this will happen if, when you are on top, you genuinely care for others. If, when you are in advantageous circumstances and authentically use your good fortune to spread good, your blessedness increases.

Sharing my good fortune increases it.

43. Resolute Breakthrough

I resolutely breakthrough and remain.

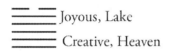 Joyous, Lake
Creative, Heaven

When you are doing the right thing, keep doing it. Creating a heavenly lake of experience is a joyous activity arising from purity flowing continually from Source. Staying one with higher consciousness is accomplished by gentle, confident inner connectedness to beauty, goodness, truth, and harmony. Know who you are; your core essence is holy and good. Your core is love. Spirit is love. You and Spirit are one. Breaking through to sacred being is happening for you now.

Feel the state of grace. Feel overall well-being. All you have done, are doing, and will do is directed toward enlightenment. Remaining on the path of beauty, goodness, truth, and harmony preserves this state of grace.

Here is a great game to play with yourself. Every time you get off center, see how fast and completely you can return to calm acceptance. Once you have become aware of a new situation, wishing it were not so won't change it; but you can change its effect. So the more quickly and completely you accept it, the more you are empowered to handle it well. Ask inside *who am I?,* and experience being pure awareness, pure consciousness.

The *Course in Miracles* teaches that our upset always comes from a false belief we have created about ourselves. Healing comes from clarifying that false belief and letting it go because it is untrue. Letting go of this self-judgment into knowing our sacred self as pure love heals.

Acceptance of what is empowers you to take the best action, to take each next best step. Outer peace comes from inner peace. The paradox of peace is that it comes from letting go of things having to be any particular way other than the way they are and proceeding from there. Profound acceptance brings profound peace.

You have arrived at a time when you know that you know right and you do it and keep doing it. This keeps you connected to Source.

Congratulations, you keep arriving into a state of greater wholeness as you resolutely persevere with gentle breakthroughs you achieve each moment.

When you lose it, all you need do is let go back into the flow of life. Appreciating that you ultimately are life, which is love, so doing, you return to breakthrough after breakthrough. Welcome home to your soul, your center, your oneness with all beings. You are love, lover, and beloved. Realizing this is the truth that sets you free.

Breathe and enjoy that you are love. Breakthrough and be free.

LINE 1: With much to do, avoid rushing or taking on too much. Proceed with one thing at a time, one thing of optimal size and pace. Do higher priorities first. You will enjoy the doing and the completion.

I remain in grace by resolutely observing optimal pace and priority.

LINE 2: Cautious considered attention prepares you for any eventuality. Being well prepared sustains clarity over reactivity. Equanimity, preparedness, and meditative flow keep you secure and whole. Feel inner peace radiating throughout all your affairs.

With careful preparation, I proceed with wisdom and peace.

LINE 3: At times you may be caught in relationship with another who is caught in lower intentions. You may not be able to immediately free yourself. Others may judge you. But that is okay when you remain correct. Slow, wise transformation of the situation or disengagement is the best course now.

I slowly and wisely change or extricate myself from untenable situations.

LINE 4: Pushy willfulness creates resistance, the opposite of what you seek. Gentle quiet confidence is the most profoundly powerful.

In gentle, quiet confidence, I transform challenge to opportunity.

LINE 5: Be resolute in breaking through from lower to higher habits. Connection within is the path. Meditation may help. Proceed with joy and confidence with this valuable change and success is yours.

I am resolute in breaking through to higher habits.

LINE 6: Success seems achieved. It seems easy. But in this exists potential problems. You may be tempted to take it easy and become remiss in the resolution to go to the heart of the matter and carry on the breakthrough to higher levels. This not being careful, allows lower impulses to gain ground and undo gains achieved. Resolute care and carefulness preserves the gains. Success is sustained.

I remain resolute in careful caring and sustain gains.

44. HIGH CONNECTIONS

I create and keep high connections.

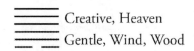 Creative, Heaven
Gentle, Wind, Wood

As wind blows things about creating change, a variety of influences blow into each of our lives, some beneficial and some challenging. It is our task and opportunity to discern the beneficial and connect only in ways that benefit all concerned or at least do no harm.

Your consciousness is precious. Nurture it and it will serve you well. Do not let it blow about at random with whatever wind comes.

As various people, circumstances, thoughts, feelings, and actions come and go, we have the power to choose which we engage and which we let go.

Embrace good rather than resist evil. Resisting negativity gives it energy. Embracing good brings light. At every turn, you have power to choose the good, beautiful, true, wholesome, and whole, as well as the kind and the gentle response. Choose wisely and you prosper in health, abundance, and wholeness. Choose the opposite and the opposite blows into your life like an unwanted hurricane.

Be kind, yet wise when encountering forces that would otherwise harm you. You will breeze through danger as though it did not exist. Stay alert, choose wisely and you benefit. Thus you transform yourself and the world.

LINE 1: Lower motivations can come into one's consciousness disguised as small and inconsequential. It is just such apparent smallness that can fool you into allowing it. But this seed can grow and become self-destructive. It is easiest to weed out negative influences at the beginning when they are small and weak.

I weed out potential negatives early before they have the chance to grow.

LINE 2: The best way to cleanse one's self of lower motivations is with gentle persistence, rather than harsh reaction, which itself is a lower motivation. While so cleansing, keep these lower elements from doing harm. Keep them from interactions with others and allow no room for them within you. You will succeed.

I persevere with ease in gentle withdrawal from lower and keep moving toward the higher.

LINE 3: There is an impulse to press on in a self-destructive process, within or without. Let go of this in favor of receptivity to what is most deeply good, wise, harmonious, kind, and loving, and you replace danger with blessings.

I release all that is harmful or dangerous moving toward the wise, loving, and harmonious.

LINE 4: Treat all people well and all will treat you well. If there are some who would pull you down with extended contact, tactfully withdraw without alienating them.

I treat all people well, tactfully withdrawing from those who would pull me down.

LINE 5: Be your best self and let life correct others through natural consequences. It will. You, meanwhile, are setting a good example and creating a good life.

I am my best self and allow others to follow their own path of evolution.

LINE 6: Withdrawing from lower elements in others and self succeeds. If one is judged for the withdrawal, that is okay too. Simply focus on the good; this focus undoes anything other than good, itself.

I gently withdraw from lower elements in myself and others and focus on good; all the rest takes care of itself.

45. Gathering Resources

I draw together the best relationships,
thoughts, and things.

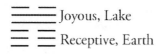 Joyous, Lake
Receptive, Earth

As streams and rivers merge into lakes, gather resources to create abundance and joy.

Relationships, things, and thoughts make a difference. Creating excellent details yields success. Spread goodwill and cheer. First, in your own heart, use every opportunity to touch the highest in you in each detail. Perceive mistakes as opportunities to learn and improve.

In relationships, build affinity, benefiting all concerned. In all you think, say, and do, create no harm. This builds a community of trust, harmony, and enjoyment. This gladdens and benefits all.

In the world of things, especially with the earth itself, be respectful and appreciative of what you have. Do your part to preserve and protect these gifts. With yourself, preserve and protect the precious being you are. Choose true and constructive perspectives in all things. You have sometimes more, sometimes less power to affect circumstances, but you do have power in how events affect you in the meaning you make of them, the perspectives, the points of view you take. In choosing constructive perspectives, you set in motion positive self-fulfilling prophecies. This creates profound positive results.

Enjoy the fruits of constructive self-discipline. Align with power for good, and right, and joy. As you let go of fear and greed into love and generosity, you create exceptional opportunities. You assure yourself a long life of love, joy, prosperity, friendship, health and wholeness. Give yourself the gift of giving. Enjoy your life. It is here for you now.

LINE 1: As a group gathers looking for leadership, leadership is shared. Leadership is passed among members depending upon the situation and the strengths of each. At times, you will be called upon to lead, at other times, to follow. As a member, be sure the leader is leading in pure ways and directions. As the potential leader, ensure the same in yourself. If these criteria are not met in either role, let go and proceed toward purity and true goodness in both means and goals.

I participate as a follower or leader only in ways that add.

LINE 2: People who are meant to be together are naturally drawn to one another. There is no need to artificially contrive things.

I know those meant to be together will naturally be drawn there, so I let go of forcing.

LINE 3: When you want to be accepted by an already formed group, it can be difficult and humbling. If the group is truly for good and therefore worth entering, there is a way to do so. The following combine over time to open the way—modestly allying with someone of stature in the group, taking a lesser position of true service, and persevering in learning how to be a valuable member of the group. All the while remain connected to the infinite within receiving wise guidance and experiencing wholeness.

I join well with others, modestly serving and allying myself with good people of good purpose.

LINE 4: You meet with good fortune and success when you work for the good of the whole.

I am fulfilled as I work for the good of the whole.

LINE 5: People gather around one in a position of influence. Some are more, some less dedicated to true service. Maintaining inner independence, truly working for the good of the whole in persevering self-improvement, you inspire higher motivation in all concerned. All benefit and things go well.

Focused on the truly good, I serve the best in and for everyone.

LINE 6: If your good intentions are misunderstood by one with whom you would like to unite, it may bring sadness and expressions of grief. This expression may help the other realize your authentic benevolence and shift to a more accepting attitude. At a certain point, it is wise to self-heal creating inner independence, and connect with others who reciprocate your goodwill, desire, and skill to relate well. Connection with the infinite within is extremely helpful in these matters.

When I meet resistance, I authentically attempt to contribute, I may express my vulnerability to a reasonable point, after which I wisely commit to others and withdraw into inner guidance and await greater receptivity.

46. Effort Now Rewarded

With gentle perseverance,
I succeed in this opportune time.

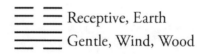 Receptive, Earth
Gentle, Wind, Wood

Wood grows upward from the earth in gentle steady progress. Effort is now rewarded as you grow toward the light. Humble, aligned, and flexible effort succeeds. Humble means holding yourself equal with, neither above nor below, others. Aligned means following good. Flexible means adapting readily, bending around obstacles. Joyfully know that what appears at first to be an obstacle, when wisely accepted and understood, is valuable information for excellence in evolving.

The path of evolution is learning and gaining new skills and attitudes from opportunities disguised as obstacles. Redefine obstacles as opportunities, and you make them precisely so.

Sometimes work and effort are rewarded. This is just such a time. So get cracking. Don't just sit there; do something. Just kidding. Before setting out, be sure to connect deep inside and listen to what, where, and how to proceed. You will succeed.

LINE 1: As you begin, create confidence. Build a strong foundation by connecting within. Allow inner guidance and love to pull you upward as the light attracts a growing plant. Stay connected to the light of love. You live in grace.

I begin in the confidence of being connected within. I am inspired to grow in the light.

LINE 2: As you begin, you learn profound ways to proceed in your environment. Success and support come with high intentions, kindness, and a solid work ethic.

I gain and sustain support and success with kindness, high intentions, and solid work.

LINE 3: Success proceeds with ease. To gain the most in this propitious time, don't ask why; just plow ahead staying connected to Spirit.

Remaining in harmony with Spirit, I steadily progress in this opportune time.

LINE 4: Honor and success grow slowly and definitely as you persevere. What you are doing is real, valuable, and most of all, aligned with ultimate good.

I receive plentiful rewards from slowly steadily making real, valuable contribution.

LINE 5: Neither celebrate success too soon, nor grieve setbacks. Simply step forward, one step at a time, with either temporary success or failure. From success, take heart. From what doesn't work right away, learn. With both, persevere in gentle progress.

I take heart from initial success yet restrain premature celebration. I accept, gently persevere, and learn from initial frustrations. I often gain more from the latter.

LINE 6: Avoid impulsive action. If one way is barred, try another and another until the way opens. With flexibility and perseverance, you stay whole and ultimately succeed.

I do and redo until I learn and achieve excellence.

47. REST

I rest and refresh into
dreams coming true.

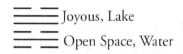 Joyous, Lake
Open Space, Water

As water fills a lake, allow yourself to fill with joy and health through deep rest. Meander like a gentle flowing stream, stopping here and there to fill pools of rest that nurture you, then, proceed. You will be fulfilled. Upon reaching the lake of rest, bask in its soothing healing waters. Bathe in its purity. Let the Divine encompass and embrace you. You have done well. You have earned a deep rest. You could use a deep rest. Take a deep rest.

LINE 1: When challenges arise, it is essential to your happiness to stay whole. The first step is to build your inner strength. With such strength, all goes well.

All goes well as I stay whole and build inner strength.

LINE 2: Even though outward things are going well, there are times in life when challenges require planning, preparation, a positive attitude, deep rest and a slow pace to succeed. You will succeed as much as you observe these steps. Keep faith in yourself, others, and connection with the divine.

This all-encompassing trust creates an aura of confidence that is the foundation of success.

I proceed with higher purpose ensuring success.

LINE 3: The way you look at things creates your feelings about them. To experience this, shift thoughts from negative to positive and see how your feelings shift with them. Look at challenges as opportunities rather than as oppressors. Your choice determines your results.

I create success by embracing positive perspectives.

LINE 4: Allow yourself the joy of giving to those who will most benefit and appreciate your gifts.

I experience the joy of giving by giving to those who most appreciate and benefit.

LINE 5: There are times when your motivation to be of authentic and significant contribution to humankind calls for creative effort that can only be done by you, and no other. Relish this opportunity to serve in loving kindness; this self-generated inspiration carries you to your goal.

I celebrate and give the gifts I have to give. This energy carries me to my goals.

LINE 6: The choice is yours. You can indulge in negativity and stay stuck or free yourself. Know you can overcome any obstacle with perseverance, positive perspective, pacing and tapping into divine will. You can be either the source of your greatest problems or your own best influence.

Since viewpoint profoundly affects existence, I embrace positive perspectives.

48. THE SOUL

I drink deeply
of pure soul love and wisdom.

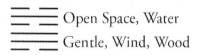 Open Space, Water
Gentle, Wind, Wood

In ancient times, wooden buckets were used to draw water from a well. Drawing water from a well represents drawing the best from deep within you. Let go of trivial things. It is an excellent moment for profound progress. What are your gifts? What is your life purpose? What needs attention most in your life now to progress along your chosen path? How? When? Where? Is it a good time to go deep within your own self or with another or others? If the latter, who?

Contemplate these things and proceed. Your life, your being, your soul are enriched.

Consciously proceed with what brings most good each moment. Feel it in your heart. Let it radiate from deep within. Patiently wait to act until you know the right thing to do. When the time is ripe, act.

Drink often from the well. Realize the better unique you. Let the inner wisdom of life itself flow from your center. Open your heart. Love, gently, warmly, wisely, and actively.

LINE 1: Focus your precious time, attention, and energy on profound matters and relationships.

I focus joyfully where greater good is to be discovered.

LINE 2: To keep and develop your purity, wisdom, and goodwill, express these attributes.

I express purity, wisdom, and goodwill.

LINE 3: You know what to do, but you are not doing it. You know what it will take to free yourself to live a life of inspiration, joy, love, prosperity, serenity, harmony, and safety for you and all you touch. Proceed to do so.

I realize and actively live my life purpose.

LINE 4: Taking time to evolve, may call for temporary retreat from directly serving others. This is all right, as long as there is intent to return to serve. You will be all the more able to do so, because of the time invested on self-evolution.

I take time within to prepare and give without.

LINE 5: Everything in your life at this and every moment is working for your and everyone's higher interest. Your task is to meditate upon joy, peace, harmony, inspiration, and purpose. Express in concert with the symphony of inner wisdom that comes as you quietly listen within. Give yourself the gift of joyfully continuing to raise yourself. Do what's better for you to do in each moment with gratitude for the privilege.

I give myself the gift of joyful continuous improvement.

LINE 6: However one listens within, be it meditation, contemplation, nature, dialogue, the *I Ching* and other writings sacred to you, pure love and wisdom are there for everyone. It is inexhaustible. It is born in connection with and integration of heart and mind, the essence of pure love and wisdom.

I dive deep within for precious pearls of life.

49. Transformation

I evolve and
the world evolves with me.

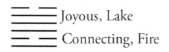 Joyous, Lake

Connecting, Fire

The image of fire and water presents two radically different entities. The fire below heats the water above causing transformation from liquid to gas. Contrasting times bring about opportunities for change which inspire personal transformation.

As you read changing times and ferret out new requirements for success, opportunities arise to elevate yourself and your world. You benefit with all shifts from lower to higher, from judgment to acceptance, from anger to forgiveness, from fear to love, from greed to generosity, from hard to soft, from guilt to compassion for others and self, from ego to Spirit. When you meditate in stillness on each of these shifts, one at a time, you receive many gifts from Spirit.

The new you synchronizes with new times. You realize opportunities. Your personal transformations present you with positive effects and effectiveness. As you respond in new and more wholesome ways, you gain momentum building health, happiness, and prosperity.

Those who knew you before and those just meeting you experience an evolving person with genuine concern for the well being of others. You draw to yourself only benevolent influences in harmony with what you radiate.

Congratulations, you are becoming new, with new prospects in a more benevolent new world you have had a part in creating. As you persevere, benefits continue to flow one after the other, each multiplying the value of what came before. Hold true to your inner evolution and experience the treasures.

LINE 1: Persevere in non-action, in stillness, in harmonious ease with all about you. No action is the best action at the beginning. Reacting to premature pressure to change is a mistake. Wait in quiet, open-minded calmness, until the obvious next step becomes so clear and energized that it flows naturally. Wait for this condition; it has not yet appeared.

I wait in quiet openness until the obvious next step arises so clearly energized that action flows naturally.

LINE 2: When things obviously need changing, do so. First, prepare. Prepare for the process of change. Conduct yourself well, once the change is made. Align with helpful people. Hold high standards of independent goodwill and detachment.

I change when indicated. I prepare, evolve, persevere, and align in nonattached benevolence.

LINE 3: Be neither too hasty nor too reluctant to change. Not all ideas need doing. Consider well in calm detachment. Let inner truth guide you. Sometimes change is for the better and sometimes not. Pay attention. Change is big and merits patient consideration. If you choose to change, proceed at a slow patient pace. Be conscious. Create excellence in self, process, and product.

I optimize the rate I change.

LINE 4: Real change, to succeed, must benefit all concerned. Then everyone supports the change. What's right and good succeed.

I change in ways that benefit everyone including myself.

LINE 5: Since what you resist persists, allow instead. When change is completely aligned with higher principles, it is intuitively known to be good by all including oneself. Now is such a time. Now is such an opportunity. Proceed.

I discern change toward good and do it now.

LINE 6: Slow, conscious, careful change is less scary and more effective. Realize more for less, the best way to proceed now.

I know cautious progress is better and proceed accordingly.

50. Ripe with Plenty

I realize my higher self.

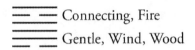 Connecting, Fire
Gentle, Wind, Wood

The fire fed by wind and burning wood underneath cooks the food. The image is presented of a cauldron filled with simmering nutritious food, the first line being legs; the next three lines, the pot; the next line, the handles; and the top line, the lid.

This abundance of nutrients encourages you to bring forth your unique gifts. Focus on your passion for good, your calling. What can you contribute most? Rather than waste time and effort on things others do better, devote your energy to doing those things no other can do as well as you. You may think there is nothing; this is misleading. Begin within, touching your soul, your spiritual connection. You will be guided to fulfill your purpose. The greater your connection within, the more empowered you are.

There is a creative essence in you yearning to express itself. Allow yourself the joy, the contribution, and the deep rewards to make your contribution to create and recreate yourself, your life, and your world.

Calmness and wholeness come on the path. Give yourself the gift of harmonizing with Spirit. Be mindful each moment. With respect for others and kindness for yourself, bring awareness of self, your deepest, highest, and best. You succeed and create joyful peace of mind.

Inner peace is a very high state. Open your heart through altruistic love. Release ego in favor of the inner peace of self-acceptance, self-mastery, contribution, and self-love.

LINE 1: Anyone in any position can grow, contribute and succeed. Turn yourself upside down and pour out all impurities. Right yourself and cultivate your highest being. Again, turn yourself upside down and let the cornucopia of your fruits pour out serving the world. All goes well.

Knowing I have much to contribute, I purify and humbly do so well.

LINE 2: With goodwill toward others, all goes well. Be satisfied to do good in alignment with the will of the Divine. Great rewards come. If jealousy comes, know that you are free of harm when you are spiritually aligned. Your sense of accomplishment will be real, deserved, and protected.

I do good for its own sake and thereby am embraced by good.

LINE 3: If unnoticed for your good works, keep working at something truly spiritual; your work inevitably will rise and be noticed.

If unnoticed, I keep working in solitude on what's truly good knowing it will be valued in the right time, place and by those for whom it is meant.

LINE 4: Come from your higher self. Relate to the higher self of others. Let those who choose to come from lower levels go their own way.

I come from my higher self and leave others to choose the same or not.

LINE 5: Remain approachable, even as you achieve high position and regard through modest ways and goodwill. Doing so brings capable assistance when you need it.

I remain friendly and modest with achievement, which brings capable assistance when I need it.

LINE 6: A spiritually inspired person following the infinite within is strong and soft and attracts all good. Great good fortune comes with this.

From spiritual inspiration, I remain soft, yet strong within and therefore attractive without; great good fortune flows from this.

51. New Energy and Wisdom

*I embrace what is
and Spirit embraces me.*

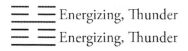 Energizing, Thunder
Energizing, Thunder

Thunder doubled energizes. Wisdom brings joyful resolution. With reverent intuition, all things turn out for the best.

With powerful energy, manifest your higher self. Accept. Clear the field of your consciousness to receive what you need to know to maintain confidence and calm. Act wisely. Exponential improvement comes as you follow and maintain higher consciousness.

In quiet meditation, listen within. Request guidance for the beautiful, good, and true. You may inquire further of the *I Ching*. By continually focusing on what's higher and seeking the gift in any challenge, you make your experience fruitful, joyful, and energizing.

Excess stimulation can come from exhaustion. With deep breath, anxiety turns to excitement. To remedy exhaustion, monitor the need for rest. Then rest sufficiently.

Excess energy can come from overstimulation. Completing smaller tasks at a slow, deliberate pace, one at a time, as part of an organized whole keeps up flow and avoids overwhelm. Suspend effort before you are exhausted. Shift huge projects into ideal size parts creating optimal challenges that joyfully lead to growth and progress. This is part of the joy of life.

Quiet your mind. With reverence, align with the Divine by calmly focusing within. You are strengthened with divine will working in and through you.

Discover your inner power. Remain wise; cease or shift any thoughts that make you a victim. An effective way to do this is to change the questions you are pondering to questions of how you can best contribute. Setting this intention puts you in a creator role.

When exhaustion and chaos come in spite of your excellent efforts, say little, say it gently, and rest as soon as possible. When a new day arrives, you will be glad of the opportunities brought by previous circumstances.

When the energy of thunder is present, focus your attention where necessary for your greatest benefit. Return to wholeness and understanding. Steer around temptations to feel mistreated. Avoid repeatedly ruminating on thoughts that put you in the victim role. Rise to higher consciousness as soon as and as much as possible, with compassion and empathy for those you would judge including yourself.

Give both yourself and others space, time, and peace of mind by expanding your consciousness within, and more physical space without. When the storm clears, bask in the caring, commitment, and mutuality that come with higher consciousness and kindness toward others and yourself.

Nurture yourself psychologically, physically and spiritually. Empower your higher nature and the greater good. Contain reactions from extremes. Respond consciously creating what you want. Have no doubt you are dealing with forces that can bring pain if left untamed. This lesson is precisely about taming yourself. You empower your higher nature and greater good the more you redirect these powerful energies to benevolent impulses.

Respond with wisdom, kindness, and compassion to others and yourself.

Whatever your situation, your social position and power, you sometimes meet frustration. How you handle frustration determines your rise or fall. This is a time of opportunity. How will you handle it? What will you do today, right now, to be a creator, rather than a victim? What will you do to be loving, kind and wise?

Bless others and yourself by transcending and transforming difficulties into growth experiences and you will gain, grow, and create the best of all possible worlds for loved ones, yourself, and all concerned. You will be big-hearted. Even more than the love coming from others, you will love yourself through experiencing true worthiness because of the good you are generating.

Forgive others, and yourself. For your own peace of mind, forgive and proceed. Forgiving does not mean condoning inappropriate behavior; rather forgiveness means accepting others in spite of their actions. Forgiveness means letting go of obsessing and embellishing the story of others' transgressions. And letting go of painting yourself as holier than thou. Forgiveness runs like a powerful current through the most successful intimate relationships.

Choose to be your best self in each moment.

LINE 1: Something that, at first, seems not okay turns out to be good. The energy of the initial impact can be used to create good.

I transform the energy of what seems initially undesirable, to create good.

LINE 2: You gain more than you thought you lost. Through nonresistance and calm acceptance, what you thought you lost spontaneously returns, soon. Focusing on losses cements them. Peaceful allowing empowers creative response and positive results.

I allow and accept, creating greater gain than that which I thought I had lost.

LINE 3: External events may take an apparent turn for the worse. Staying calm and alert empowers you and transforms this crisis into opportunity.

With calm clarity, I transform apparent setback into gain.

LINE 4: When you resist circumstances, you resist your own good. When you allow what is, you free yourself to create greater good. Allowing is to actively take the perspective that everything happens for good reason and proceed to discover then harmonize with that reason. You benefit.

I benefit from allowing and actively taking the perspective that everything happens for good reason. I am free to creatively respond.

LINE 5: Although thunder may be present, you stay centered in calm wholeness and forward movement because of the higher levels of consciousness you are achieving. Experiencing your arrival at these higher levels is reward in itself and incentive to keep going and reach still higher levels. On balance, these gains far outweigh the challenges that inspired your transformation. There is no loss, only gain.

I remain steady in challenging circumstances transforming myself and circumstances, and thereby realize great gain.

LINE 6: When inner thunder prevents the peace of mind necessary for discerning and doing the right thing, the best next step is to go within and be still. If others are involved and sense the composure you have gained, it may be a challenge for them. They may judge or test you. Give them and yourself sufficient distance from their reactivity and you will be free, whole, and happy.

I give myself quiet composure in difficult circumstances by inner focus with stillness. If this draws another's judgment, I give us both time and space, which brings harmonious resolution.

52. Meditate

I listen within in stillness.

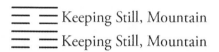 Keeping Still, Mountain
Keeping Still, Mountain

Congratulations. With this reading, you are invited to enter Divine consciousness. The guiding image is a gentle, rounded, still, serene, mountain. In inner stillness, you receive inner light, wisdom, and joy.

Stillness is allowing non-motion. Letting go of motion in your body supports letting go of motion in your mind. A restful body releases stress and becomes a fertile field for the mind to similarly rest. Sometimes it helps to precede deep rest with a vigorous physical release of exercise, a work session, or a walk to enable such a quiet body and mind. Stretching and yoga may be helpful. Focus on four simple words, here, now, clear, whole. Then focus on gentle natural breathing.

In quiet body and mind, thoughts slow down and may even cease. Slowed or stopped, the mind opens. Open space is created to receive, sense, and hear the quiet inner voice. A soft, upright-seated posture undoes kinks and facilitates the flow of life throughout the core of your central nervous system, your spine, and brain.

What will you sense or hear? You often will hear or intuitively know, all is well. How can this be?

All is well because all things happen for good reason. When you attune within, you receive precise guidance for playing your part each moment. Rushing ahead, trying to impose your will over what was meant to be, you decrease your connections with inner guidance. At first, gentle reminders attempt to inform you. When you listen and respond wisely, all goes well. If you do not, increasingly painful consequences come until you get back on the path of greatest flow and most gain. This is not punishment but ultimately loving guidance for your own and others' benefit.

A gift of optimism is that it relieves you of the stress of feeling you have to do it all, to figure it all out, now, and impose your perspectives on others. Excessive pushing promotes pushing back.

Now is a time to be still. Say little and say it softly. Absorbing inner guidance brings abundant peace. Your role is to listen for higher guidance. Enjoy the process, the beauty and fruits of higher consciousness.

When you welcome higher guidance within, all goes well without. Approaching life with a quiet, open heart and mind, you open to the divine. The divine has the interest of all at heart. All includes, yet is not limited to you and your loved ones.

From inner quiet, you create the best possible outcomes. Be still and listen within.

LINE 1: In the beginning, when things are innocent and peaceful, it is an excellent time to receive inner guidance. With the confidence of inner knowing, set your sights for smooth passage from now into the future.

Now and evermore, I remain open to inner light and guidance.

LINE 2: Align with what's good, right, and true. In this be determined by your higher self rather than by others' alternate agendas. Be friendly, yet firm, consistent, and wise. Let your actions do your talking.

I align with the Divine in quiet inner determination to follow my higher self.

LINE 3: Align with higher self and higher purpose, not by holding tighter but by letting go into beauty, bliss, and harmony. Release negative thoughts, intentions, and actions. Cleanse your consciousness of judgmental debris. Then you are filled with light, presence, and peace supporting wholeness, health, and happiness. It brings wealth of all nature and knowing that all is becoming as it should be. From this alignment, all things improve.

I purify my consciousness opening space for my higher self to lead.

LINE 4: Let go and know all is well. A body at rest creates a mind at rest. A mind at rest aligns with the Divine. Come from the perspective that all is as it should be and you realize it is so.

In quiet, I realize all is well.

LINE 5: Say little. Say it gently with wisdom, kindness, and optimism. Let your actions speak the language of love.

I say little, and I say it gently. I let my actions speak the language of love.

LINE 6: Every effort to still your mind nourishes you. You find success in putting at rest all worries. Open yourself to infinite wisdom through deep quiet within. All beings feel your wholeness and tranquility, and at their level of ability, resonate with the inner peace you radiate. Great good is yours now.

I realize the vast value of quieting my mind I and do so.

53. REVERENT STEADY PROGRESS

I immerse in reverent steady progress.

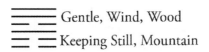 Gentle, Wind, Wood
Keeping Still, Mountain

A tree on a mountain top gradually puts down deep roots and thereby withstands the wind. Bring about serenity and benevolence by carefully attending to details. Allow yourself to become completely absorbed in creating the beautiful, good, and true. In non-reactivity, goodwill, and wholeness, focusing with complete concentration, you know joy and emerge whole.

These are excellent times to enjoy slow careful work.

LINE 1: Great works are created in stages, not all at once. Accept slowness at the beginning, for slowness with careful attention creates excellence.

I take tender careful steps at first.

LINE 2: Beginning successes are accomplished. Calm equanimity to carry on well is established. Sharing good fortune multiplies it.

I welcome a competent, steady, satisfying flow and share in its rewards, multiplying the benefits.

LINE 3: Pushing ahead too fast, coercing others, or holding them in blame, all ends unsuccessfully. Sustain a calm, centered, grounded, whole, steady presence, allowing matters to evolve at their own pace and all goes well.

Without blaming others, I allow the slow steady pace that brings progress.

LINE 4: At times you may find yourself in challenging situations not of your own making. You remain blameless by maintaining equanimity and harmony. Following this path, things work out for the best and you gain in character and enhanced relationships.

I persevere in calm and compassionate response to whatever arises, and thereby gain and grow.

LINE 5: As you progress, others seeing you rise, test you to see if they can pull you down. Such trials, met with wise graciousness, enhance you.

As I respond graciously with wisdom to tests of success, I am enhanced.

LINE 6: Wholeness comes naturally with completion. You achieve your goals. Peace and contentment fill you. Your good works are a beacon of wisdom and trust in life. All is extremely well.

I gently complete, which brings wholeness, fulfillment, and inspiration to others and myself.

54. AFFECTION

I live the purpose
of deep joyous caring.

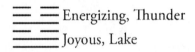 Energizing, Thunder
Joyous, Lake

Relationships can hold a lake of joy, meaning, and energy for you. Yet at times, the energy can be too intense. There is great joy in resolving issues in relationships remaining calm and whole. Look below the surface; go to the heart of matter where we are all human. Find and honor true mutual interest. What core goals do you share? Who do you want to be? To others? To yourself?

Life sometimes adds to your growth and therefore, your good by putting relationship exercise equipment in your path. Allow this assistance from Spirit with an open heart and mind.

Spirit is all good, all knowing, and all powerful. You can trust that facing challenges well brings benefit. Your relationship with Spirit is always whole and complete. You need only make peace with what is to find ultimate peace within and without. Sometimes making peace requires changing your circumstances.

Life provides you with ups and downs, challenges and rewards, and opportunities to expand by providing circumstances for you to improve. Nowhere is this truer than in the real world of soul-to-soul relationships where who you are and how you treat others and yourself makes a real difference. Rise to the challenge. Enjoy giving the gift of loving.

Two things bless relationships—being self-sufficient and being present when called. A balance of both generates mutual trust and affection.

Be gentle and genuinely kind. Respect interests and opinions of others; listen deeply with a quiet heart and mind. Make no negative judgments of that which to another is wisdom or sacred. Relate with harmony and goodwill. When all will benefit, share your own ideas and values without self-judgment.

Intend good for all. Co-create with the Divine and each other. Follow the path of least resistance; it is always there. This is the place where everyone benefits and thus supporting agreements in both the making and the maintaining. This path is ultimately the easiest, highest quality, and most enduring.

You have arrived at a time when all relationships support you because you support the best for all. Preserve this precious peace of mind; it is of the highest value.

Enjoy harmony in all relationships. To harmonize, consider the reality of the other. Simultaneously observe and maintain proper boundaries gently. Make it okay for you to see things differently than others; this goes a long way to harmonize relationships.

Maintain inner and outer harmony by adjusting social distance from intimacy to cordial depending on circumstances. And enjoy life. It is here for you. Go slowly. Savor precious moments. Unite with your higher self.

Blend well with others. Create good for yourself and others whose lives, hearts and souls you touch. Find and feel the best in yourself and them.

Keep feeding your soul by expressing loving kindness. Be secure in this wise guidance. Let the light of love always be most dear. Wisdom is gained from the past. Keep the fires burning by feeding the fire of loving attention for yourself and others. Bless all living beings.

Receive great blessing. Live in loving presence. In expanded being, hold yourself and others sacred.[13]

LINE 1: Background positions can be more fulfilling and nurturing than the limelight when embraced with joy, humility, and serenity.

With joy, humility, and serenity, I realize the soft connectedness of private intimacy as deeper than the limelight of fame.

LINE 2: Focus only on good, and all goes well. Be gentle and kind. Integrate the best for all concerned with those present or absent. Follow the Divine. Align with what is and you will know harmony within and without.

My soul sings in inner and outer harmony with all that is beautiful, good, and true.

LINE 3: Sometimes one may pursue a path inconsistent with higher values. Self-esteem returns with the return of higher motives.

Through perseverance, I constantly return to wholeness, joy, and meaning.

LINE 4: Allowing life to develop slowly and naturally nourishes relationships. This creates deep worth and fulfillment. Savor the steps. Create high quality in all things. Accept when it is time to go slowly. Know you are creating value with patient perseverance.

I allow life to develop slowly and naturally, which fulfills me both with others and myself.

LINE 5: Whatever your social position, do not focus on your own purposeful designs, but on loving kindness, wisdom, and joyous compassionate equanimity lighting your way. Advancements come from constant improvement. Relish being creative in your own life. At each stage, use available resources to create greater gains. Sometimes you must wait for issues to resolve. Focus elsewhere to give others and circumstances time to evolve. In the meantime, you are free to evolve on your own.

In patient perseverance, I allow others and circumstance time and space necessary to come to creative completion.

LINE 6: Embrace relationships and agreements of substance over form. Find deep agreement within and between hearts and minds in co-authorship with the Divine with what's good and right, gentle, and kind. One meaning of sacrifice is to make sacred. Make sacred your own life. Align with what's beautiful, true, and good and genuinely serves and protects the best interests of all. Let things unfold naturally and gently in their own time, in sacred time.

Allowing things to unfold naturally and at their own pace brings me fulfillment each moment.

55. THE SACRED STEWARDSHIP OF ABUNDANCE

As I share, savor, and save
in sacred stewardship, I expand
all abundance.

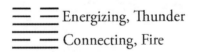 Energizing, Thunder
Connecting, Fire

Fire energized by thunder brings clarity as bright as the sun producing abundance. It is a time of profound power, influence, and prosperity for you.

Such abundance is short-lived, so enjoy it to the fullest while it lasts, and be unattached as it wanes.

The quickest way to undermine abundance is to hold it in self-centeredness. Radiate your light upon all who welcome it. Remaining abundant comes to those who realize abundance is divine stewardship given for the purpose of benefiting all. Abundance arises from goodwill in good works. To keep abundance flowing, continue to share. To continue experiencing joy and well being, notice what's going well and keep doing it.

Peace of mind in oneness with the divine brings abundance. Appreciating all that is good in your life strengthens you to transform challenges to opportunities thus feeding your soul.

Line 1: Over time, clear understanding and hard work by two or more creates abundance, prosperity, and joy.

I participate in team effort bringing abundance.

Line 2: Redirect envy and mistrust to wisdom and love. There is profound fulfillment in creating good for all concerned.

As *I redirect envy and mistrust to wisdom and love, I realize profound fulfillment.*

Line 3: When you encounter others living at lower levels, allow them to be as you hold firm to your higher nature. Over time, your light inspires them to transcend their darkness.

I allow others to live without judgment or interference. I hold firm to the highest self I can be each moment. Over time, this has the benefit of inspiring others.

Line 4: You advance with wise action. Move to a higher plane. Good fortune.

I advance with wise action.

Line 5: Being open to good advice and excellent assistance propels progress.

I accept and grow from excellent advice and assistance.

Line 6: Your lasting wealth is wisdom, love, and authentic goodwill for all. As you let go of pride and selfishness into sacred stewardship of resources that are presently in your hands, you are spiritually and materially more abundant.

As a living part of the whole, I embrace sacred stewardship in my relationship to all that exists. This sacred stewardship increasingly fulfills me.

56. Disarming Exploration

I explore and engage
with wisdom, care, and caution.

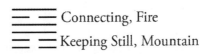 Connecting, Fire
Keeping Still, Mountain

Like a settled old mountain, not steep and jagged but gentle, curvaceous, and lush, cling to inner quiet, peaceful thought, and right action. In new territory, it serves well to blend in, watch, and learn.

You are exploring new things. Offend no one. Be gentle and forgiving. Avoid conflicts. As quickly as possible, resolve any issues that arise.

Limit yourself to only your higher nature. Take no offense. Do not submit yourself to extreme tests now. Be easy with everyone. Avoid potentially harmful people, places, and circumstances.

Savor your new willing boldness to explore the unknown. Yet do not expect those who are established in power and influence to hold your perspectives and accommodate your every wish and command. As you accommodate them, you are welcomed. You are giving birth to a new life. Be careful and caring at this moment while others are forming lasting first opinions of you.

Relate to present circumstances as sacred opportunity.

LINE 1: Be and stay whole by granting the same to others. Radiate goodwill toward all. Express goodness from your heart, mind, and feelings in all speech and action. You have the power to choose and manifest who you are. Reserve your precious attention primarily for those higher connections that nourish your soul most deeply.

I choose wisely what, how, and with whom I invest my attention.

LINE 2: Modesty and right action wins loyalty of others. Excellence, humility, kindness, and wisdom encourage others to support you.

With humble presence and kindness, I attract dear friends.

LINE 3: Return to innocent present presence. Ego, arrogance, and meddling in the lives of others lose support. Opening to inner guidance avoids pitfalls. Life, once again, nurtures you.

In plain presence, I cultivate calm.

LINE 4: Though you are safe and stable, anxiety may remain. Stay correct in heart, mind, and deed. The time to act is not yet. Wait in wholeness. You will know when to move forward. All will proceed harmoniously. Know all is well and will be well.

I let go of worry and stay pure. I know when and how to proceed. All goes well.

LINE 5: Holding quiet love within for all, you are a stranger to no one. From this gentle place, find and follow local custom. At first, you will be accepted, then welcomed, and finally celebrated and loved.

I am a stranger to no one. I follow accepted custom, which opens doors to community.

LINE 6: Lowering stress serves you, your purposes, and your community. Replace reactivity with flexible, gentle presence.

In calm acceptance, I evolve my relationships and myself.

57. CALM HEALING PROGRESS

I act with subtle, gentle power,
energizing and integrating
positive perspectives.

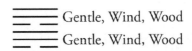 Gentle, Wind, Wood
Gentle, Wind, Wood

Wood comes from small seeds becoming great trees with slow calm progress. Over time, a gentle wind continuously blowing in a single direction has great influence. With gentle ease and steady forward progress, you experience success after success.

At the quantum level, thoughts have just as much physical reality as a rock or a table. The particles of thought are just farther apart which makes them more pervasive and therefore ultimately more far-reaching and influential. The beautiful thing about thoughts is that when they are negative, they are exquisitely easy to change to replace with new positive thoughts. These new positive thoughts carry more power than the negative. Light comes to the darkness, bringing joy and success to those who have chosen the light via positive perspectives.

For example, if you have a lot to do, rather than thinking thoughts that bring on feelings of overwhelm, break complex tasks into small simple steps. Doing simple steps one at a time at an appropriate pace and taking the the time you need for rest and contemplation sustains progress. Form pleasant thoughts about each step, contributing to the bigger picture of your life purpose and meaning. You are choosing joy over depression.

Much experience is filtered through thought. Great power comes from the subtlest effort of directing your thoughts constructively. Following this path, you are using the great leverage of love. Psychologically, spiritually, and materially, your consistent thoughts influence your experience. As you shift to the positive, replacing fear with love, consciousness rises. You evolve. You experience *"higher lows and higher highs"*.[14]

Humans in history with unstoppable success and wisdom have known and lived by this subtle, powerful principle. Creativity begins in the heart and is filtered through the mind in the form of inspired visions. Gently expanding thoughts in positive, productive directions is a profound source of spiritual evolution.

Keep replacing any negative thought with a constructive thought. Each time you catch a negative idea seeking roots in your soul, rethink it in the most constructive perspective you can credibly create. It can be like inverting a fraction. For example, switching the thought, *I am getting sick* to *I am getting well.* Or in more detail, *the symptoms I am experiencing are providing valuable information such as signs that I am detoxing, or that I need and deserve rest or other beneficial treatment. With this information, I can and will be healthier. My symptoms are evidence that my healing feedback system is working well.*

You can master your life. Each thought you think in the direction you want to go propels you there. Herein is the wisdom that realizes intentional self-creation and leads to desired destinations. You become a conscious creator, the artist of your own life, the author of your soul's expression.

LINE 1: Vacillating falters. Make steady forward progress, allowing moments for rest.

I realize steady progress alternating between calm flow and recharging rest.

LINE 2: There may be subtle doubt that hampers you. With the assistance of wise counselors, including your own intuition, doubt transforms to wise discernment and resolution. All is well.

I overcome doubt with wise counsel.

LINE 3: Once you have deliberated to the core of an issue and know the right course to take, further deliberation is counterproductive. It is time to act taking the necessary steps to make higher existence real.

Through careful consideration, I discern the right course of action and proceed.

LINE 4: Persevere in building understanding and moving forward with care and modesty. Good fortune results.

I move forward with humble wisdom gained from experience and the resulting understanding.

LINE 5: Although there were some problems at the start, you are now in a position to proceed. Contemplation of what went well and what did not will guide you both before and after making valuable shifts. Once everything is smoothly functioning, maintaining the valuable changes retains harmony and success.

I integrate wisdom from experience.

LINE 6: Pushing ahead when things back up only deepens despair and decreases progress. For a good outcome, retreat, regroup, rest, and evolve.

When things get difficult, I hold back and renew proportionately.

58. Mutual Joy

I participate in mutual joy.

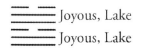 Joyous, Lake
Joyous, Lake

Like a spring-fed lake, joy feeds itself. See and feel joy springing from within, and share it. From rain, rivers, and streams of joy without, joy is multiplied within. There are opportunities for inner and outer joy to flow between you and others, and fill each of you now.

Feed others' souls and your own with the better attitudes and activities available in this opportune time. Align with all good. Spend time with like-minded people who embrace work and contribution with a sparkle of goodwill and a bold focus of adventure in everyday challenges.

When outer adversity comes, shift it to opportunity; transform it; transcend it.

Attune your soul to appreciating the fine things of life. Harmonize and be in rhythm with people, conditions, and events. Be of goodwill, good cheer, good works, and good ways. Add. Don't detract. Jump in. Join. Solve, resolve, and contribute. Quietly do your part without requiring acknowledgement. Higher order pleasures go on growing and growing. These become the heart of your experiences. You know goodness and self-love. Loving yourself brings greater health because you are in the center of healing energy. You will love yourself for worthy contributions.

Harmonize with those about you. See through their eyes that you are a creator of good. In all things good, jump in and lighten another's load. Joyfully co-create with them for the greater good. You progress profoundly. Others appreciate you. You are welcomed into community. Your hearts silently sing together. Bliss is yours in co-creation and contribution

When others test your resolve for joy by applying negative pressure, don't react; respond. To respond, choose what nurtures everyone, rather than judge others or yourself. Such judging sets in motion destructive actions based on negative emotions. Respond wisely by giving others and yourself the space and time for nonreactivity, so they see their testing is unnecessary. Allow them to choose a new joy and co-creation to whatever depth they can. Watch as they rechoose and reenter relationship from a higher, lighter place.

Avoid judging others. At the same time, discern what is good in the other and lovingly support this aspect. This uplifts everyone and everything and brings joy to all.

Avoid judging yourself. Heal negative beliefs about yourself by forgiving *mistakes*, and learning and growing proceeding forward and upward.

In the meantime, proceed in your own life with joy and peace of mind, pacing yourself to be and do well in each moment. Enjoy the inner and outer music of your soul.

Double joy within and without, with others and with yourself. Double joy is yours now. As you choose this, accept what is with no forcing. Embrace inner detachment, strength, and purity. Proceed with gentle goodwill. Outwardly co-contemplate what's higher. Be part of a spontaneous field of joy for all who choose to enter therein.

LINE 1: Quiet inner contented joy without attachment to things being other than they are is the best way to proceed now. By defining what is as okay, you create inner calm and contentment. This way you free yourself from having to have things be different than they are. You decrease suffering and expand.

I accept and remain whole.

LINE 2: Avoid practices and perspectives that do not agree with what you know to be higher. Hold fast to your deeper and better values. Joy springs from strong connection to inner wholeness and connection to radiating divine energy.

I follow the higher, better course.

LINE 3: Free yourself of dependence on externals. Avoid seductions that rob you of ultimate joy. Fill yourself within. Focus quiet attention inward. Keep connecting to Source. You build joy and wisdom. Feed yourself this life-giving attention.

I feed myself quiet, life-giving, loving inner attention.

LINE 4: When you make the choice to change from lower pleasures to working for the good of the whole with non-attachment to results, you make permanent peace and joy your own. Conflict dissolves when you follow the inner light.

I live in peace and joy when I choose to work for the good of the whole without attachment.

LINE 5: Make your inner home in goodwill, harmony, and positive perspectives, thus freeing yourself into joy and creativity. If you flirt with negative ideas or situations, you get caught in the downward energy. Instead of allowing people and things pull you down; pull them up by living simply in your high self.

I pull myself and others up by living from my higher self.

LINE 6: Find joy directly within the right and good. Forgo the seduction of seeking acknowledgement outside. Vanity imprisons one in need for outside validation to be whole. Self-worth comes from determination through inner sensing good and acting accordingly. You save your freedom, your joy, your wholeness, your life.

I follow right and good for the direct experience of joy, rather than for outer acknowledgement.

59. Gentle Healing Dispersion

*I gently heal through
soft dispersion.*

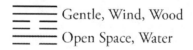 Gentle, Wind, Wood
Open Space, Water

Water evaporates into vapor. Gentle winds clear away hardness. Disperse hard attitudes. Move easily and smoothly.

Release and melt barriers with things such as soft music, spiritual practices, and cleansing visions. Swing on a hammock. Play with a puppy. Spring up and spring clean. Make music in your soul. With the soles of your feet, dance. Laugh, and sing.

Let your ego take a vacation. How? Contemplate *what can I give,* rather than *what can I get.* Forgive past mistakes: yours and others. Retain only the wisdom gained.

Meditate. Contemplate. Whisk away unwanted energies on a cool breeze. Disperse worries. Bathe your body in clear clean water. Bathe your soul in visions of a crystal clear spring, energizing freedom and health.

Be soft and receptive to all that is good. Savor life. Then life serves you.

It is time to nurture yourself with goodness. Go inward in quiet presence to depths beyond thought, beyond cares, beyond worries where whispers of the infinite soothe you. Stay until you are more than full.

Whatever worries you have, burdens you are carrying, grudges you are holding, let them all go. Let the broad shoulders of the Infinite carry any of these burdens. Disperse the rest.

Fill with warm loving attention from your higher self. Fill so much that joy effervesces in renewed life energy. Release all negativity into wholeness. Will you give others the space to be as they are? And the gift of a refreshed you? Will you give this gift to yourself?

LINE 1: Disquieting thoughts undo unity within and without. It is easier to soften sooner before the embellishing negative thoughts. Use divine leverage to make simple shifts to the comfort of knowing that all things come for spiritual purposes. One purpose may simply be to increase your power to make such shifts.

I soften at the beginning.

LINE 2: You are building a case in your mind supporting harsh judgments of others and/or yourself and/or the circumstances. Continuing on this path will imprison and bring you down. Compassion for others and self, seeing that you have acted similarly in the past, opens your heart. You are the greatest benefactor. It is a crucial matter, as the closed heart strangles the life of its owner, not only spiritually, but physically. The armored heart is a root cause of heart disease and heart failure. Open-hearted acceptance heals the heart. Accepting the humanness of others and the situations you meet in daily life brings joy, health and love. Embracing what is with goodwill is one key to healthy life.

I accept our humanness and have compassion for others and myself.

LINE 3: At times one may become caught up in a great and worthy task. To achieve this goal, it may be necessary to dissolve filters that keep others at a comfortable distance. The worthiness of the goal brings the strength to do so.

I gain strength to persevere pursuing good works from knowing the worthiness of my effort, even when it is hard.

LINE 4: Consider effects on the larger community. Entertain broad open-minded understanding. The pivotal understanding is to realize that what you create comes back to you. Creating benefit for many, you're not only supporting the whole, but also your own higher good. Transcend the false dichotomy that self and others' interests are opposed.

As I bless others, I bless myself.

LINE 5: Expand a great idea, like evolving win-win to all win. Expressing all win from a position of influence creates profound possibilities for resolving crises and advancing human evolution.

I am open to better ideas.

LINE 6: Removing yourself and others harmoniously protects all. Keeping distance from danger effectively dissolves the danger.

I effectively resolve danger by removing myself.

60. WISE RESTRAINT

I observe wise limits.

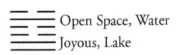 Open Space, Water
Joyous, Lake

A lake is bounded; water is boundless. The lake is defined by its boundaries. This limitation creates meaning, identity, and purpose.

The person who has no boundaries dissolves. Self-chosen limits strengthen. In the moral sphere, not engaging in unsavory activities cultivates character. In the economic sphere, restraining excess spending creates solvency and prosperity. In the physical sphere, limiting energy expended interspersed with regular periods of exercise, rest, sufficient sleep, and limiting yourself to healthy foods builds strength, health and success.

The Chinese word for limits is similar to the word for joints in bamboo. These repeated joints limit the stress on each section giving the entire length of the shaft strength with lightness and flexibility. You can be strong, light, and flexible by adopting wise, moral, and healthy limits.

Simplify difficult tasks into easy steps. Focus and refresh to do the best in each phase.

Limit your actions toward others to the appropriate ways they want to be treated. Gain the moral stature to lead and to love by restricting your thoughts, words, and actions to honor the dignity of others.

Knowing and following your limits, financially, physically, and in relationship, brings abundance, vitality, and joy.

An overflowing river creates chaos. Just as the banks of a river direct its current and flow, reasonable restraints empower personal expression. An unrestrained person can hurt others, relationships, and self.

Just as each word in a language is limited to its definition, its meaning, each person gains definition, meaning, and identity by living within the bounds of high character and the unique person they were meant to be. Paradoxically, living within limits does not limit you; with constant improvement, it empowers you to become an increasingly better person with your unique heritage, learning, interests, and visions.

Yet limit even limitation. Excessive restraint holds back creative expression and free-flow. Still, embrace valuable limits and they embrace you.

With appropriate limits, beauty arises from your unique being attracting acceptance, welcome, and love from others.

LINE 1: Use discretion. Sense when obstacles are giving you information to either stop altogether or to wait and build resources.

I discern messages from life's experiences to stop or wait.

LINE 2: Limit both beginning and hesitating. Wait for the right time to act, but no longer. Stepping on the brakes and the gas at the same time brings stress. Stepping on each in its own right time you get safely where you want to go in the best timing.

I wisely alternate stopping and going.

LINE 3: Limiting yourself to wise, right, and good keeps you safe and happy. Overindulgence brings negative consequences. You get to choose. Choose again.

I limit myself to wise actions; I under-indulge.

LINE 4: Harmonize with natural laws and limitations. For example, gravity pulls water downhill while warmer air rises. Observing natural limits opens the way forward. When one path is blocked, accept it, and you will remain whole. Find and calmly proceed where the way is open.

I harmonize with life's yeses and nos. When one way is blocked another will open.

LINE 5: Before limiting another, observe the same limits for yourself. You become wiser in setting those limits through your experience. And your example inspires greater loyalty and less resistance.

Before limiting another, I practice those limits myself.

LINE 6: Excessive limitation brings resistance. Be gentle, yet firm, when necessary. Stop judging yourself for past mistakes; instead, learn and grow from these mistakes, and you will succeed. With others, let go of the past in kind forgiveness. Be joyful, present and wise.

I hold myself back within valuable, but not excessive limits.

61. INNER TRUTH

I discern beauty, goodness, and truth
and act accordingly.

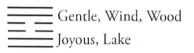 Gentle, Wind, Wood
Joyous, Lake

The image—two receptive lines in the middle of two active lines above and below—represents a heart and mind open to truth within. This is a profound time calling for utmost care in what you do and how you do it. And it is a time of opportunity calling.

Proceed slowly, graciously, and wisely with great consideration of all people and information, and you will make great decisions that will benefit everyone and everything. With such care, you will prosper, be happy, and leave a legacy of great contribution. You create the truth that you did the right thing in the best way. The beauty of such decision-making is that it lasts and nurtures everyone, including you.

This is a good time to listen inside and out. Let your higher nature interpret what you receive. Thought reinforces itself, so find and follow higher perspectives. You find peace within and contribute to creating peace in the world.

Congratulations, your conscious consideration has created this opportunity. Continue with the same graciousness. All will be well.

LINE 1: Stay connected to inner truth, to the Source of your wholeness. Any secret alliances, plans, agendas, factions, disconnect you from truth. Disconnecting from truth disconnects from the divine. To stay connected, stay true to all others and yourself. The divine is love. Staying true to the divine requires loving kindness. The truth of love empowers the inner light of wisdom creating success in all things.

I stay connected to divine wisdom through love, openness, inclusiveness, and truth.

LINE 2: Inner alignment with high or low is communicated near and far. Your intention flows through the energy field connecting everyone. The door to this field is the heart. All beings know subconsciously what you hold in your heart. You are greeted and treated according to what is in your heart.

When you focus on higher things, you attract like response. Mutual nourishment is assured. Dwelling in anger, doubt, or other negativity is communicated and known by all intuitively. Those you would want near will stay away. Others will be tempted to test you. Remaining on higher planes draws positive influence and connections.

I discern in my heart what is highest each moment; I align with what's higher and remain there.

LINE 3: Create your own wholeness. Inner truth and wholeness comes from inner independence. Be your own person. You have the choice to be elevated, lowered, or unaffected by others. The *I Ching* makes no judgment on this choice. Deep bonds of affection raise you up; that is not an error. At the same time, dependence on others for self-worth is an error because absence of regard by the other then leads to despair.

You can create your own wholeness by making goodness itself be your fundamental source of wholeness. Enjoying affinities is not wrong if you are independent when they are not present. Make your primary source be true good. With mutual goodwill and affinity, connect. Without it, give yourself and others room to be all right. Always stay connected to the divine.

My primary relationship is with good itself. I am independent of others and relate to all with goodwill.

LINE 4: To stay connected to the power of inner truth, humility is a must. Someone who *already knows everything* leaves no room for learning. Wisdom comes from receptivity to inner guidance. After achieving something because of following inner guidance, it may be tempting to forget its source. The ego loves to take credit. The paradox in so doing is you lose the connection to the degree you take credit. Maintain connection by maintaining openness and humility; all goes well.

I remain humble in the light of wisdom and continue to receive wise inner guidance.

LINE 5: Good character equals right action. Right action attracts support and agreement. Right actions come from manifesting good intentions for all.

I hold good intentions for all, which generates right action, which generates good character.

LINE 6: Promises and positive words have negative effects when right actions are missing. First study the action to know if it is right.

Beyond words, I contemplate and fulfill right action.

62. Details

Doing details joyfully and well,
I bring about heavenly reality.

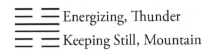 Energizing, Thunder
Keeping Still, Mountain

Thunder on the mountain seems so close, almost like it is inside you. The strong lines in the center surrounded by receptive lines signify being firm within and flexible without. It is a time for careful attention to details. Focus on small things well, and you succeed in the big picture. It is time to do details rather than make sweeping reforms. Quiet inward focus harmonizes your efforts.

Advance, yet avoid entanglements, by doing the small tasks. The strength to make monumental advance is not present now. Hold back now and prepare for such steps later. Remain outwardly cordial. yet detached.

Mastering the mysteries of life results from synchronizing ideal activities with the nature of the time. Agreement with what exists brings success. It is a good time to do little details that are harder to get to in times that support greater strides.

Congratulations, you do not need to push hard now. The best consciousness is simple inner peace. This is auspicious. Relish and savor it. Putter, play, and inch along in serene sanctuary. You can create your own happiness. Setting modest goals, filling your time with excellence in small things, success and joy are yours.

LINE 1: Practice excellent timing. Wait for right moments to act or let go. Avoid forcing change before it's time or holding on afterward; doing either creates misfortune. Inner receptivity in quiet listening to the infinite creates clarity.

I flow, in excellent timing, sensing, and doing or waiting as is ideal each moment.

LINE 2: The specifics of what to do are not yet clear. Calm acceptance with willingness to wait creates the best attitude to create success now and ultimately. The best course of action now is nonaction, staying aware for clarity to spontaneously arise.

I calmly await awareness to illuminate the best next step.

LINE 3: Proceed with extreme caution now. Be wary of excessive self-confidence. Persevere in proper reserve. Be astute, check details in accord with intuitive sensing, and all will be well.

I now embrace the excellent watchwords—limited, humble, and cautious.

LINE 4: Pushing hard obstructs opportunity. Being flexible, receptive, and gracious when things or people are not immediately receptive paradoxically opens the way. Holding back without, resolution within, move things ahead. Time and wisdom ease your way.

I am humble, approachable, and adaptable without while determined within, knowing time, and receptivity support progress.

LINE 5: Because your intentions are the highest, you receive assistance from the best hearts and minds. Graciously seek help in modest openness.

It will be forthcoming. You may find what you need in the writings of others, personal conversations, and connecting with the infinite within. Meditative calm consistency creates your fondest dreams coming true and the self-fulfillment of your making profound contribution to your world.

I attract assistance with humility and flexibility without and determination within, as I embrace higher purpose.

LINE 6: Excellence comes in small stages. Pushing too fast reverses progress. Embracing joy each moment realizes what is most desirable.

I embrace small steps with joy, transforming what is to what may be.

63. Milestones

After completing one step,
I prepare for each next step
with joy and wisdom.

 Open Space, Water
Connecting, Fire

F ire under water makes steam. Steam is power. Turn the heat up
too high, and the water boils over and puts out the fire; nothing
is produced. Turn the heat down too low, no energy, no fire; nothing is
produced. Continue at an optimal pace, neither too fast nor too slow.
Prevent problems from doing too much too fast or too little too slowly.
Avoid celebrating too soon or stopping after completing initial steps.

Take satisfaction, energy and inspiration from completing difficult
and important tasks; just don't get stuck there.

Pace yourself for the long run. Discern best options. Sense what body
and soul want. Keep progressing step by step. Make the most of your life.
Add to what's good without attachment and then final results take care
of themselves. Avoid the great impediment, a closed mind that says you
can't. If you tell yourself you cannot do something before you begin, or

It's too hard, or *It's their fault,* you will prove yourself right. Keep an open mind and heart.

To prevent excess expectations and exhaustion, be reasonable about how much you attempt at one time. The optimal approach for any task of significant size is to break it into small steps that assure success. Then proceed. Take each step in turn. Keep stepping until you reach your goal. Take valuable well-spaced rest periods. Enjoy. Smile inside and out as you enjoy the journey.

Love the good and transcend the negative. Allow yourself to be inspired with an open heart and mind. Dive into life. Love others. Love improving life. From this, you will love yourself.

Bury your ego in the bliss of contributing to others, your world, yourself. Ignite your spirit with opportunities. Keep positive thoughts alive. Know that things will work out for the best using positive self-fulfilling prophecy. Have a willing Spirit that does not sit back and expect to be spoon-fed. Give yourself wisdom and energy to constantly progress with well-paced work and optimism. Move into your higher self by focusing on the good of the whole.

You have completed much to this point. Continue, inspired by your own efforts and successes, knowing you can continue to do well.

Let the infinite within embrace and celebrate you, and carry you along the path of least resistance. Chant gently within, *I know I can, I know I can, I know I can,* and you will.

Congratulations on becoming your higher self, connected to the Source of wholeness, happiness, fulfillment, contribution, and prosperity.

LINE 1: Going crazy with plans does not create progress. Progress comes with levelheaded thoughts and smooth action.

I progress with levelheaded thoughts and smooth action.

LINE 2: Your reputation and social power wax and wane with events. Control your response. Remaining modest, focusing on higher things, and your worthiness and wellness increase.

I remain humble focusing on higher things and success takes care of itself.

LINE 3: If, after completing projects close to your heart, one lowers standards of how to treat others, gains are lost. Continued care, cordiality, and quality continue success and expansion.

I continue to treat others well even after I have accomplished gains and avoid the self-deception that the gains will remain if I do not.

LINE 4: Things may be going along well and suddenly some unhandled issue may arise as an apparent setback. Transform this to a breakthrough by going straight into what needs careful attention and bringing completion. Then all will truly be well, even more so than before.

When new issues arise in the midst of success, I handle them well and continue the success.

LINE 5: Spirit sees deep into the true motives of the human heart. Humble and true intention to be generous, kind and good has everything to do with authentic Spirituality while elaborate expressions of ego, very little.

I remain authentically humble, loving, and caring, doing good for its own sake.

LINE 6: Having successfully completed navigation of a dangerous situation, you may be tempted to refocus on it, to bask in thoughts of how well you did to the exclusion of present tasks calling for precious attention. This can bring back problems that were once resolved. The most empowering way to proceed is to attend each present moment, simply feeling confidence from previous successes but not reenergizing details that trigger emotional reactivity.

I feel self-confident from resolution of previous issues without getting caught in the details. I focus on the present task.

64. PERSEVERE

I persevere to completion.

 Connecting, Fire
Open Space, Water

With water below moving downward and fire above moving upward, these two natural forces tend to move apart, which calls for caution.

You have done a great amount of good work. You are near the end. Stay focused, persevering in right thought, attitudes, and actions to completions. Veering off into complacency or doubt undoes what's done. Completing with careful attention fulfills dreams coming true.

Proceed with the caution of an old fox moving over ice. Be cautious and alert to signs of cracking ice, of problems arising in the direction one is taking; adjust accordingly. The young fox is impulsive and may get wet by overreaching. Be aware and responsive to natural indicators and forces as you complete your journey.

Notice the rhythm as you move up the hexagram; alternating first to receptive, then to creative lines. This is the optimal cycle for proceeding. First, be receptive, sensing circumstances clearly. Respond creatively to what you sense. Proceed wisely with each step.

Persevere in steady considered progress to complete what calls. Listen within and sense without. Integrate the wisdom gained into purposeful action. Discern the better paths and destinations and follow through.

Use momentum that arises as you approach completion. Be wise with the strength of flexibility to constantly evolve your vision with feedback.

Wait until you get go signals within and without; when you do, move forward in joy knowing success is assured because of the care with which you are proceeding. You are mastering life.

LINE 1: Be well prepared before beginning action. Starting too soon limits quality. Holding back at this time helps. Tempered consistency creates the highest quality and sustains vitality to complete over time.

I proceed with moderate speed that supports excellence.

LINE 2: The time to start is not yet, but soon. Be ready. Get yourself and things in order. It may take some study and self-improvement or some rest, so when it is time to proceed, things will flow.

I prepare well and consciously and patiently await the right moment to begin.

LINE 3: It is time to act, but you lack the power by yourself to accomplish the task. If you push ahead alone, a setback will occur. If you seek assistance from excellent sources, other people of skill and goodwill and the Divine within, you succeed.

In the right time to begin, I proceed with the best support available.

LINE 4: You are grappling with the challenge well. Keep going. You will do very well if you stay at it with your present purity of effort. Beware of decadent attitudes setting in and upsetting your progress. Look back with great satisfaction on the great results you created through steady self-application.

I sustain purity in my effort.

LINE 5: You've done it. You have completed magnificently, and the rewards are all the greater because you persevered so well through the challenges. Congratulations again. If you doubt this, stay focused and the sense of success will come. You are a light to the world, a center of appreciation from without, but ever more so sweetly from within.

I savor the rewards of pure effort.

LINE 6: Forego ego swelling with success and stay modest. Things continue to go well. Enjoy the successes. Just stay humble and you will secure gains accomplished.

As I remain modest, gains are sustained and grow.

NOTES

1   From podcast at TaraBrach.com. This site is filled with inspiring talks.

2   By Robert Cooper in "The Other 90%". Quoted by Brian Johnson at PhilosophersNotes.com.

3   How does this dissolving of reactive feelings work? Perhaps you have heard the phrase *the map is not the territory*. If we have a map of Costa Rica, an abstraction, it is not Costa Rica itself, the reality. The false self, some call the *ego*, the reactive small injured innocent part we experience, comes from the stories we tell ourselves; the abstractions, not the real alive self living anew in each moment. By asking and experiencing, who is it that is injured, we shift to experience our real live self, our connection to Spirit, instead of the story, that activates the reactive emotions. This direct experience dissolves the ego reactivity, and protects us psychically because we have shifted from identifying with the abstraction to identifying with true life itself, our connection to Spirit, all life, wisdom, love, and energy. Here are two ways to dissolve the ego and connect with the real self. The first, as explained above, is to ask and experience the experiencer, the real live self. The second, when you are assisting another to overcome reactivity, is to listen with total caring presence, and no content or agenda whatsoever, for the person being listened to. At first the person will release the stories, and then they will get in touch with their real live being and its connection to life itself, to Spirit. From this will flow insight and healing. This is the essence of the best psychotherapy as eloquently explained in the book, *Thoughts Without a Thinker* by Mark Epstein. The first way of making the shift can be experienced instantaneously; the second takes some time. Both have infinite value.

4   Thank you, Alana, for this wisdom. Taken from a personal experience with Susan and David Butterfield of the transmitted beings, Alana and Legion, creators of the Heart Room, a set of teachings in Learning How to Love, and how to Welcome Change with Love.

5   Thank you to my Great Aunt Amy Loomis, an advanced spiritual teacher, for sharing the alone to all one transformation in consciousness.

6   Thank you to Brian Johnson of PhilosophersNotes.com for sharing this big idea from Wayne Dyer's brilliant book, *The Power of Intention*.

7   Thank you, Alana, for this wisdom. Taken from a personal experience with Susan and David Butterfield of the transmitted beings, Alana and Legion, creators of the Heart Room, a set of teachings in Learning How to Love, and how to Welcome Change with Love.

8   For more on Coasting Uphill, see Theo's blog at TheoCade.com

9   Thank you, Martha.

10   It's much easier to balance on a bicycle or surfboard that is moving forward at a reasonable speed.

11   From Tara Brach's talk on Happiness at Tarabrach.com.

12   See *Choose Again*, published by the Center for Attitudinal Healing, Vancouver, BC, and Costa Rica. Available through *www.choose-again.com*. This is the most effective and empowering emotional release and clearing approach I've found in over 50 years of studying psychospiritual evolution

13   Namaste is a greeting that honors the sacred within the other from the sacred within you. Live this wisdom.

14   Quoted from Brian Johnson at PhilosophersNotes.com.

Hexagram Key

Upper ▸ / Lower ▾	Heaven	Thunder	Water	Mountain	Earth	WindWood	Fire	Lake
Heaven	1	34	5	26	11	9	14	43
Thunder	25	51	3	27	24	42	21	17
Water	6	40	29	4	7	59	64	47
Mountain	33	62	39	52	15	53	56	31
Earth	12	16	8	23	2	20	35	45
WindWood	44	32	48	18	46	57	50	28
Fire	13	55	63	22	36	37	30	49
Lake	10	54	60	41	19	61	38	58